PNG ELEMENTARY ENGLISH PROGRAM

ELEMENTARY ONE

STUDENT BOOK

TANDI JACKSON

OXFORD
UNIVERSITY PRESS

Oxford University Press is a department of the University of Oxford. It furthers the University's objective of excellence in research, scholarship, and education by publishing worldwide. Oxford is a registered trademark of Oxford University Press in the UK and in certain other countries.

Published in Australia by
Oxford University Press
253 Normanby Road, South Melbourne, Victoria 3205, Australia

First published 2011
Reprinted 2013, 2014

ISBN 978 0 19 557472 2

Edited by Sandra Balonyi
Illustrated by Uramina and Nelson
Typeset by Kerry Cooke, eggplant communications
Printed in China by Golden Cup Printing Co. Ltd

TABLE OF CONTENTS

WEEK 1

Exercise 1A

Say this chant to your friend, pointing to the words.

Ant on an axe   a   a   a

Axe on an ant   Aaaaah!

Exercise 1B

Look at this house.

Draw it on paper and colour it in.

Colour the roof red.

Colour the window yellow.

Colour the wall green.

Colour the door black.

Exercise 1C

Read this to a friend.

This is a house.

This is a door.

This is a roof.

This is a window.

This is a wall.

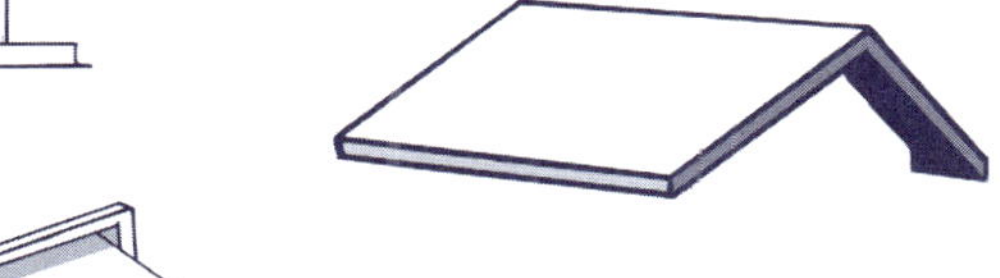

Exercise 1D

Put a stone on the picture that is different. Do this with your teacher.

Now draw the different ones.

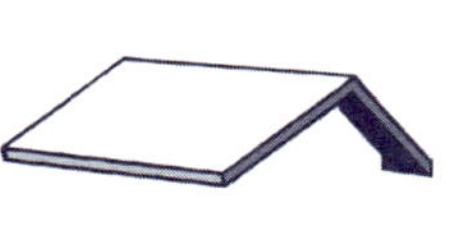
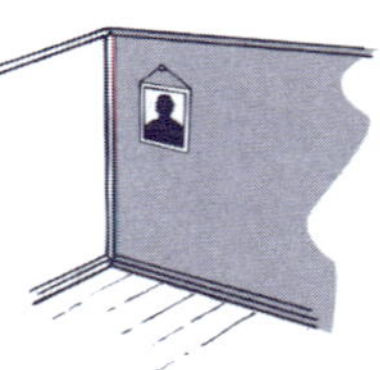

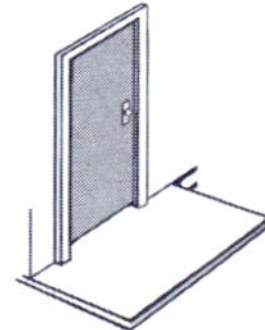
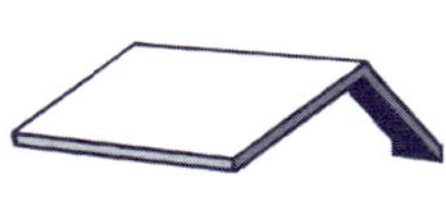
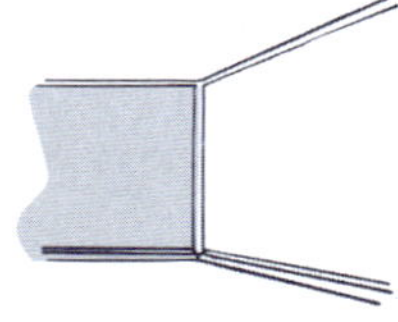

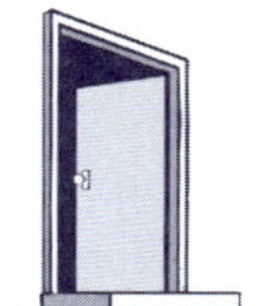
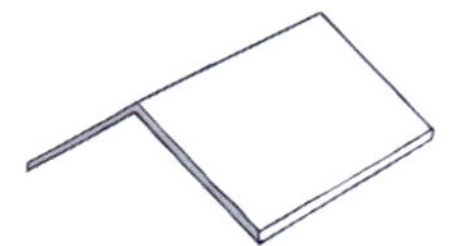

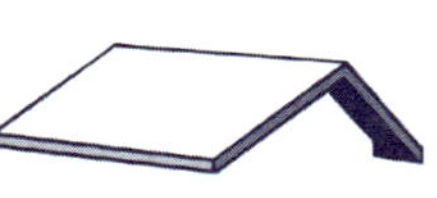

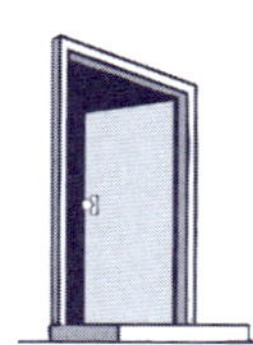
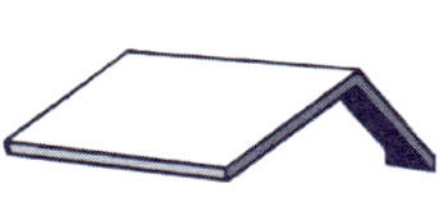

Exercise 1E

Find the big one. Say the names in English.

Exercise 1F

Say these words. Can you use them in sentences?

a   an   at

WEEK 2

Exercise 2A

Say this chant to your friend, pointing to the words.

Baby in a bed **b b b**

Bed on a baby **Wah! Wah! Wah!**

Exercise 2B

Point to each building or place and say its name.

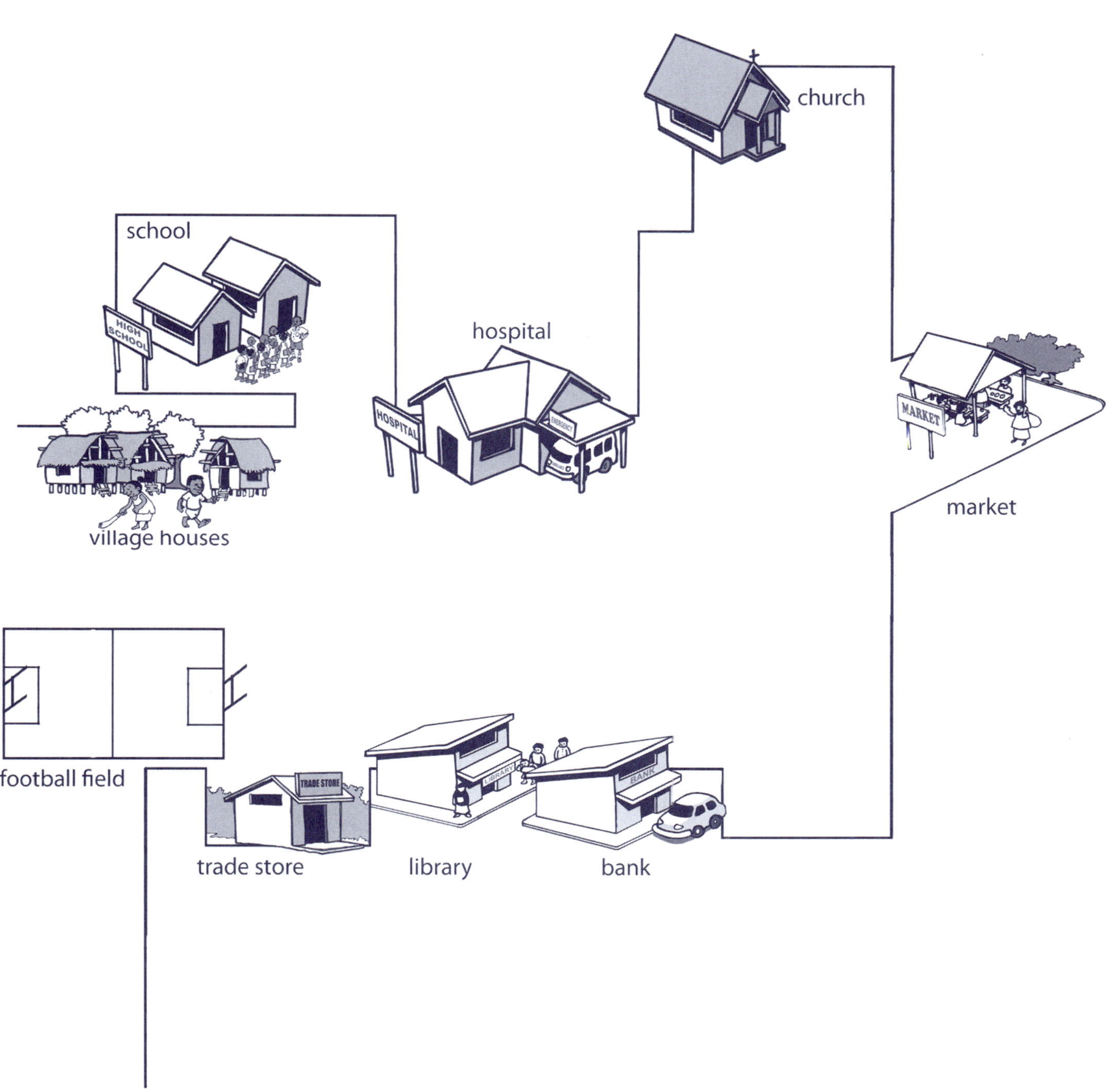

Exercise 2C

Read these sentences.

This is a big truck.

This is a big hospital.

This is a small bike.

This is a small house.

This is a big church.

This is a big school.

Exercise 2D

Read these sentences.

My village is big.

My house is small.

My school is big.

The school library is small.

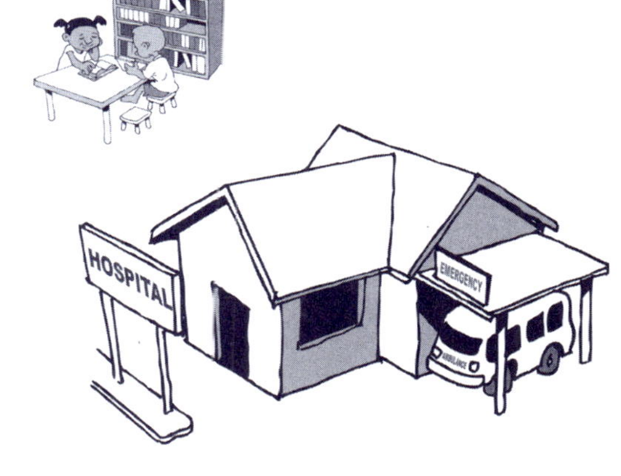

The hospital is big.

The trade store is small.

Exercise 2E

Can you say these words to a friend?

big	boy	by

WEEK 3

Exercise 3A

Say this chant to your friend, pointing to the words.

Cat on a car **c c c**

Car on a cat **Miaow! Miaow! Miaow!**

Exercise 3B

Draw the transport used in your local area.

truck

car

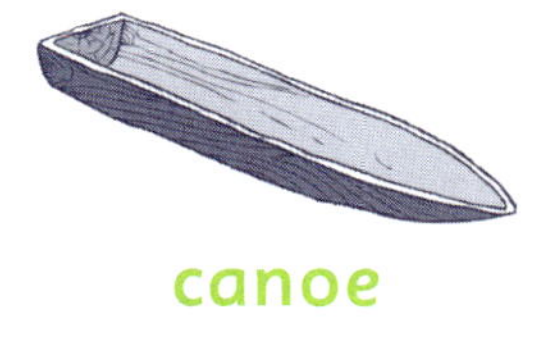
canoe

plane

speed boat

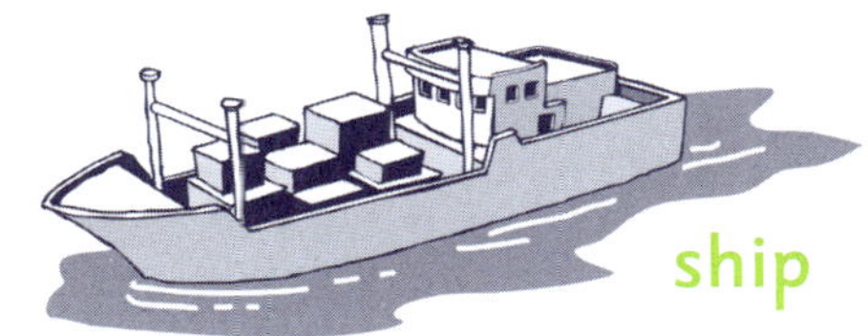
ship

Exercise 3C

Fold your paper in half. Draw the things that go fast on one side and the things that go slow on the other side.

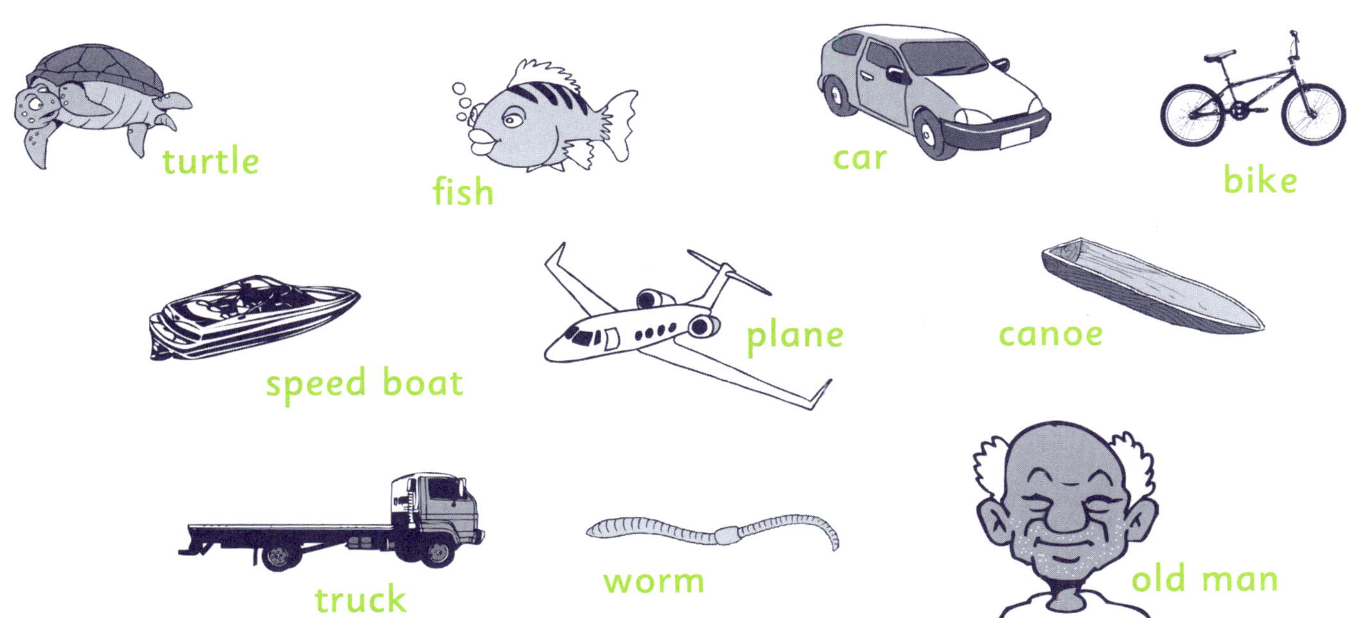

Exercise 3D

Look at the race. Draw the one that came last on your paper.

Exercise 3E

Read these to a friend.

My car goes fast.

A truck goes fast.

A plane goes fast.

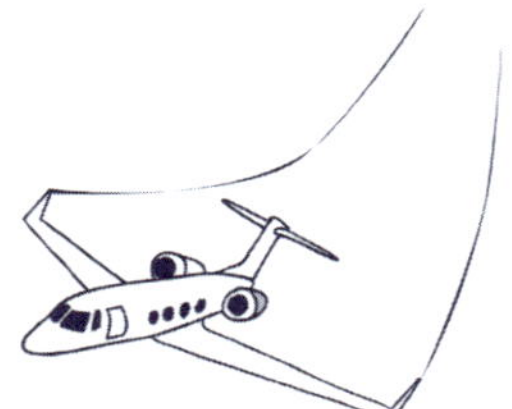

This truck goes fast.

This boat goes fast.

This motor bike goes fast.

This bus goes fast.

Exercise 3F

Draw the big ones.

a big truck

a small boat

a small plane

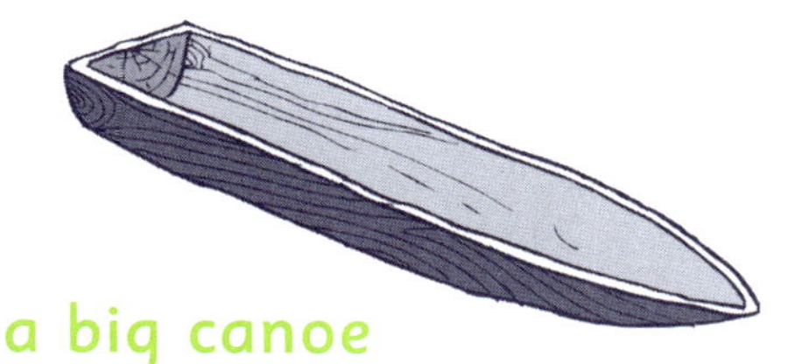

a big canoe

a small car

a big bus

a big plane

a big boat

Exercise 3G

Say these words to a friend. Can you say them in sentences?

can	come

WEEK 4

Exercise 4A

Say this chant to your friend, pointing to the words.

Dog on dad **d d d**

Dad on a dog **Ruf! Ruf! Ruf!**

Exercise 4B

Match the food on the bottom that comes from the things on the top. Draw them on your paper next to each other.

 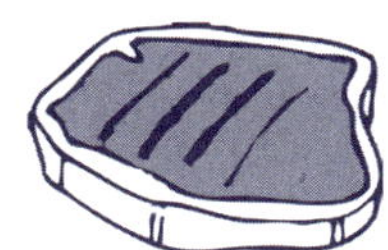  

Exercise 4C

Read these sentences to a friend.

I see an ant, on an axe.

I see a cat, on my car.

I see a baby, in the bed.

Exercise 4D

The things on the left are living things. The things that are made from them are on the right.

Copy these pictures onto your paper. Draw lines from the living things on the left to the things on the right that are made from them.

The first one is done for you. Do not write in this book.

Exercise 4E

Copy these pictures and choose the right word to go with each picture.

dog   dad   door   dig

Exercise 4F

Fold your paper in half. On one side draw the living things and on the other side draw the non-living things.

Exercise 4G

Say these words to a friend.

door   dig   did

WEEK 5

Exercise 5A

Say this chant to your friend, pointing to the words.

Eels on eggs **e e e**

Eggs on eels **We're swimming in the water!**

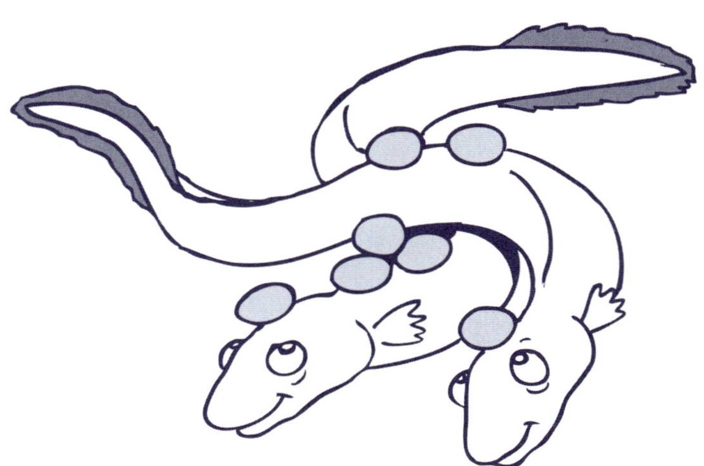

Exercise 5B

On your paper, draw the things that plants need to grow.

Exercise 5C

Read these sentences to a friend.

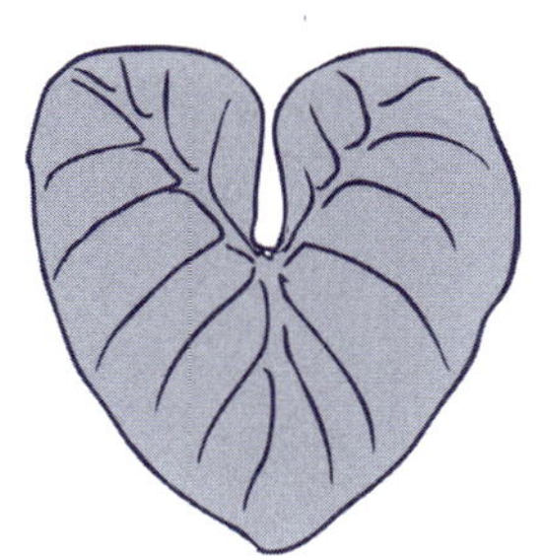

This is a taro leaf. It is big.

This is a flower. It is red.

Look at the beans.

Look at the red flowers.

Look at the big seed.

Exercise 5D

Can you read these words? Say them to a friend.
Now find word cards that match.

an	big	can	door
eat	at	by	come
dig	boy	car	every

Exercise 5E

Draw these pictures on your paper in the right order.
What do you do first?

Exercise 5F

Draw the fruit or vegetable with the correct seeds next to it on your paper.

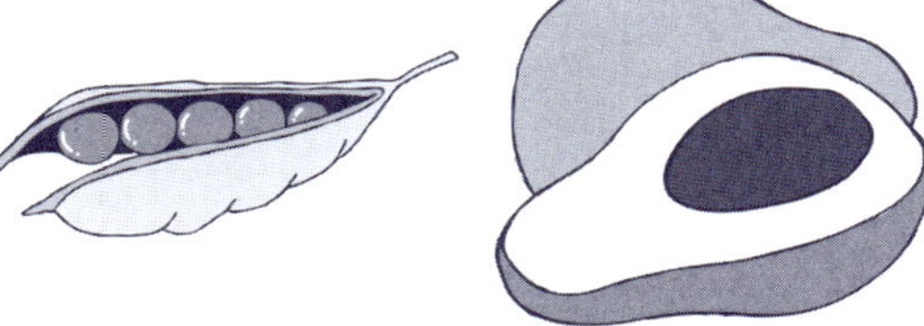
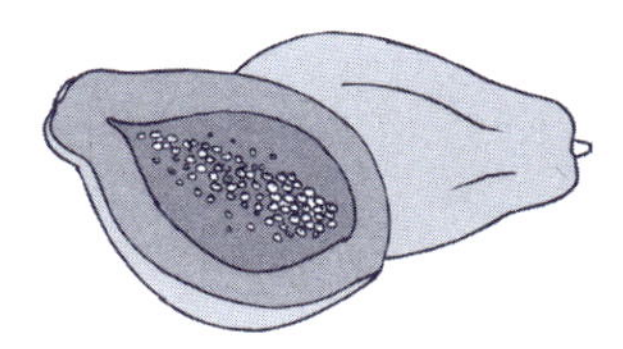

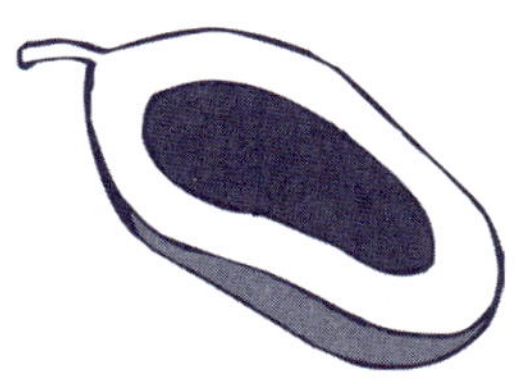

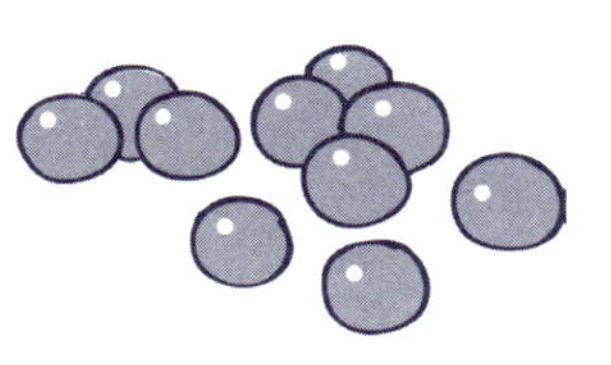

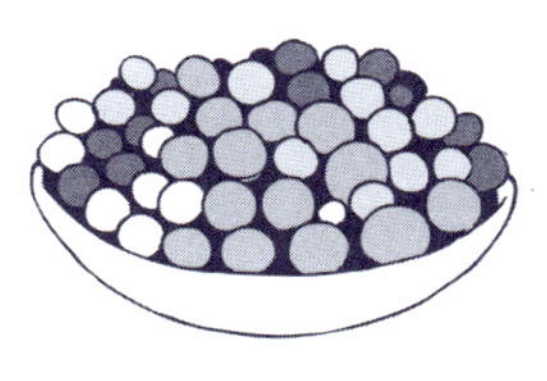

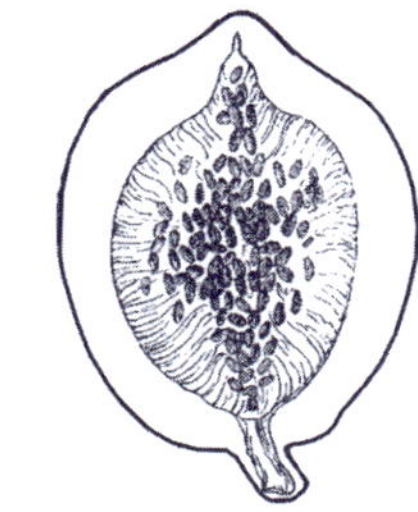

Exercise 5G

Say these words and then draw the pictures on your paper. Tell your friend a story using these words.

beans

sun

rain

flowers

leaf

soil

WEEK 6

Exercise 6A

Say this chant to your friend, pointing to the words.

Ant on an axe a a a

Axe on an ant Aaaaaah!

Baby in a bed b b b

Bed on a baby Wah! Wah! Wah!

Cat on a car c c c

Car on a cat Miaow! Miaow! Miaow!

Dog on dad d d d

Dad on a dog Ruf! Ruf! Ruf!

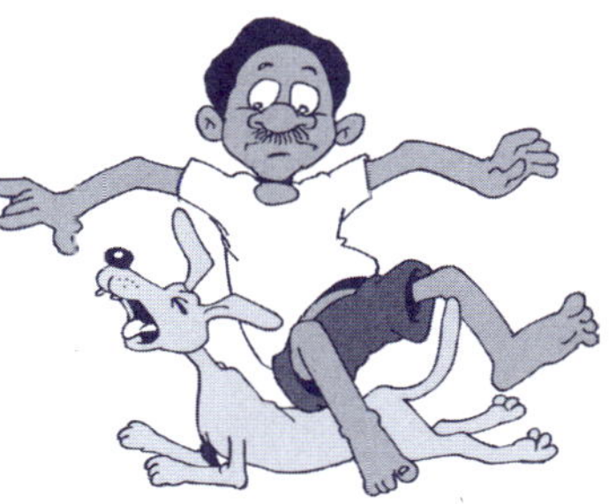

Eels on eggs e e e

Eggs on eels We're swimming in the water!

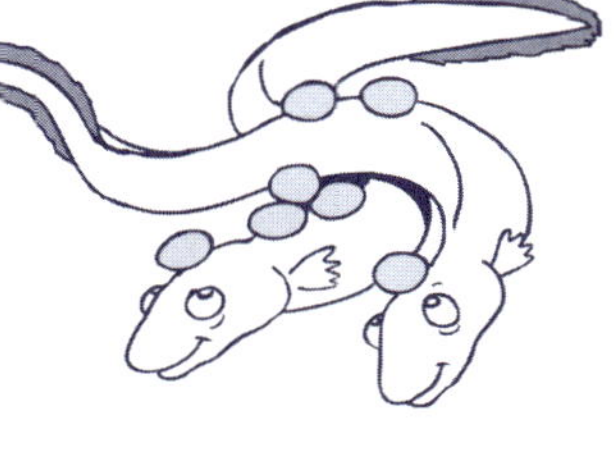

Exercise 6B

Say all these words and draw the pictures for them on your paper.

ant	axe	baby	bed	car
cat	dog	dad	eels	eggs

Exercise 6C

Fold your paper in half. Draw all the vegetables you like on one side of the paper and all the ones you don't like on the other side.

Exercise 6D

Put these letters in the right order. Write them in your exercise book.

e a c d b

Exercise 6E

Which of these are ready to plant? Draw them on paper.

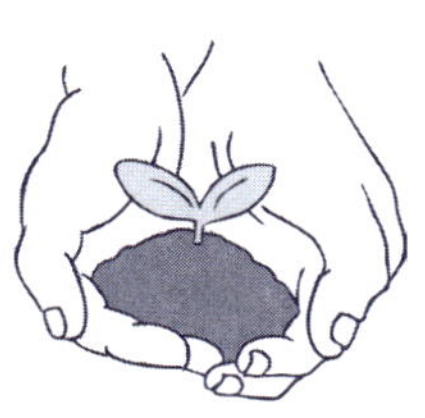
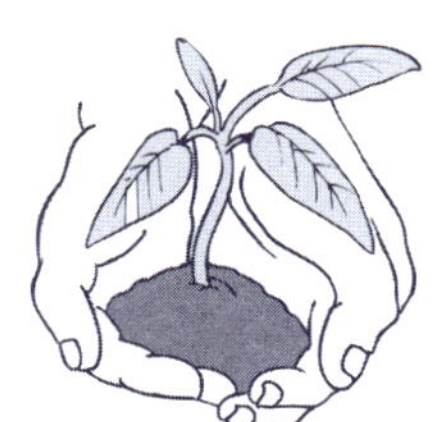

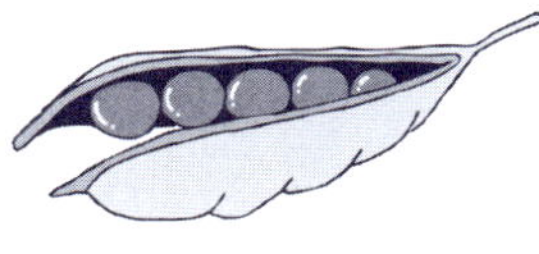

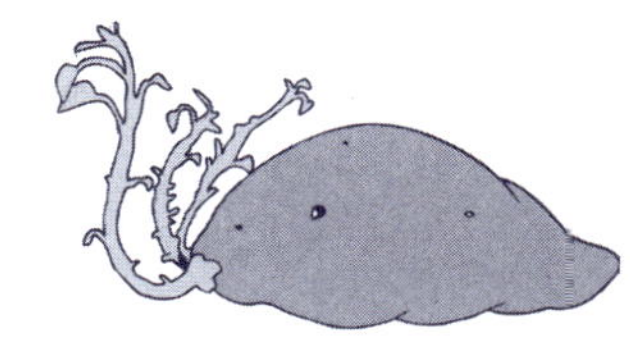
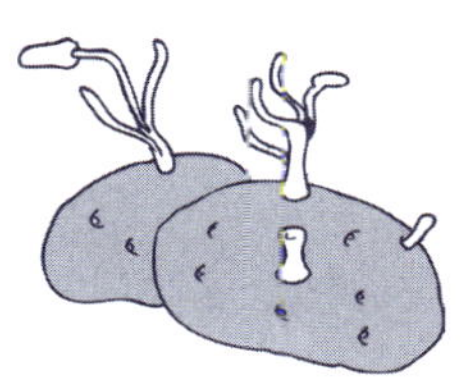

Exercise 6F

Say these words to a friend.

dig every come a

by at boy can

door eat be an

WEEK 7

Exercise 7A

Say this chant to your friend, pointing to the words.

Fly on a fish **f f f**

Fish on a fly **Shoo fly, shoo!**

Exercise 7B

Draw the fruit that grows in gardens in your local area.

Exercise 7C

Put a stone on the fruit in each row that is the same as the first one. Draw it.

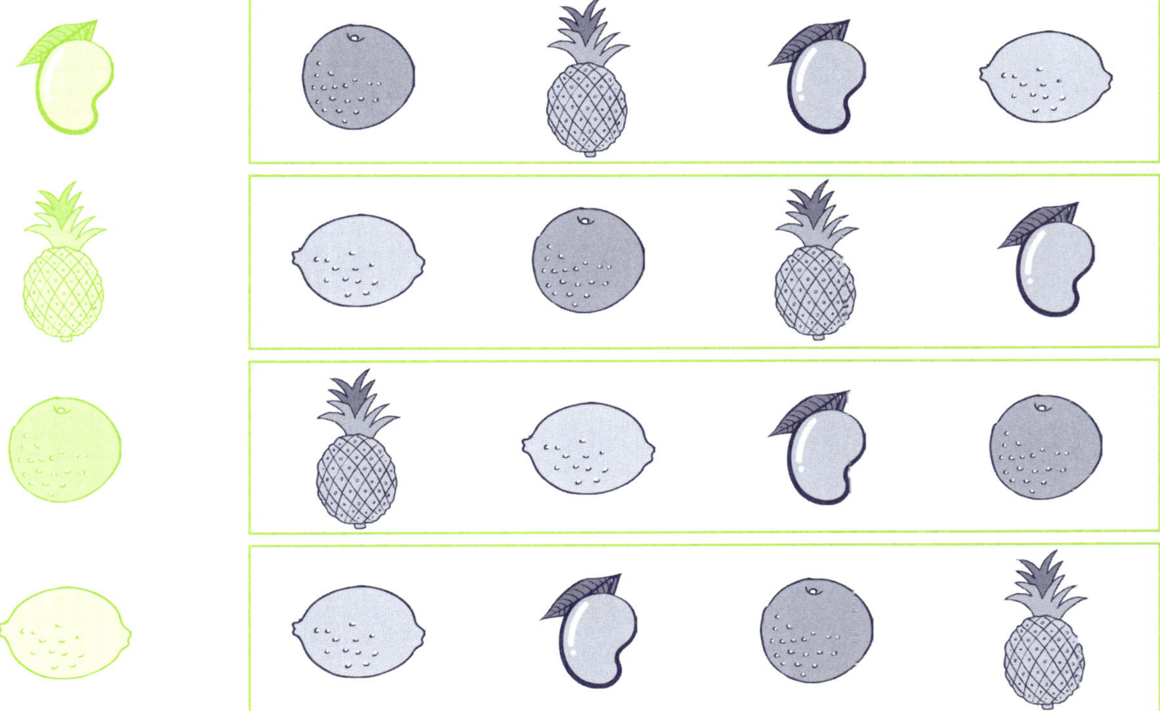

Exercise 7D

Draw these fruit trees on your paper and draw the correct fruit on them.

Exercise 7E

Draw the half leaf that matches with the first one.

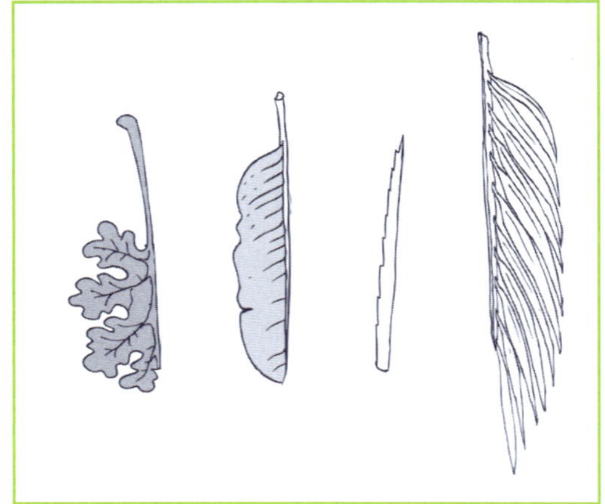

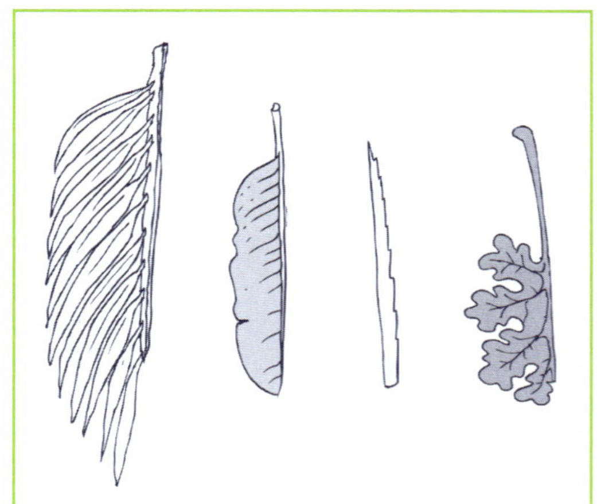

Exercise 7F

Put these leaves on the right tree. Draw the leaf and then draw the tree next to it.

Exercise 7G

Read these sentences to a friend.

I like bananas.

I like mangoes.

I like coconuts.

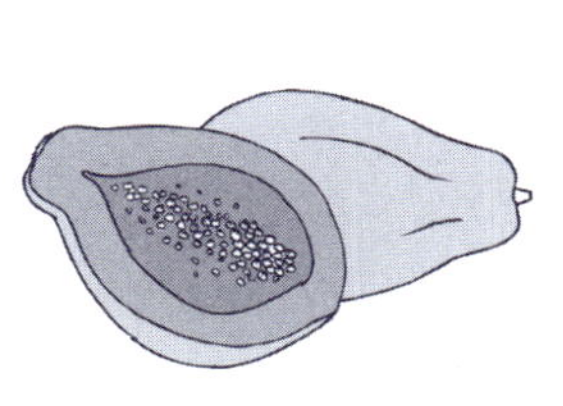

I like pawpaws.

I like oranges, but I don't like lemons.

I like mangoes, but I don't like pineapple.

WEEK 8

Exercise 8A

Say this chant to your friend, pointing to the words.

Girl on a goat **g g g**

Goat on a girl **Get off me!**

Exercise 8B

Find the right food for each animal. Draw the animal and the food next to it.

Exercise 8C

Fold your paper in half. Draw all the tame animals on one side and all the wild animals on the other side.

Exercise 8D

Who lives in the tree? Draw a tree on your paper. Now draw all the animals that live in the tree.

Exercise 8E

Read these sentences to a friend. Point to the words.

I can run fast. I am big.
I start with c. What am I?
I am a cassowary.

I am fat. I am big.
I start with p. What am I?

I am a pig.

I am small. I can miaow.
I start with c. What am I?

I am a cat.

I am very small. I eat rubbish.
I start with r. What am I?
I am a rat.

I am big. I eat grass.
I start with c. What am I?
I am a cow.

Exercise 8F

Where would you find these? Draw them in the right place in a big picture.

WEEK 9

Exercise 9A

Say this chant to your friend, pointing to the words.

Hat on a horse **h h h**

Horse on a hat **Very very flat!**

Exercise 9B

On your paper, draw all the insects with wings and say their names.

Exercise 9C

On your paper, draw all the insects in **Exercise 9B** that can bite you or sting you.

Exercise 9D

On your paper, draw the insect in **Exercise 9B** with eight legs.

Exercise 9E

Read this poem to a friend.

A big black spider,
Climbing down the thread.
A big black spider,
Landing on my head.
Shake, shake, shake my head!
Shoo! Go away!

Exercise 9F

Find all the butterflies and draw them on your paper.
(The others are moths.)

Exercise 9G

Draw the insects that are camouflaged.

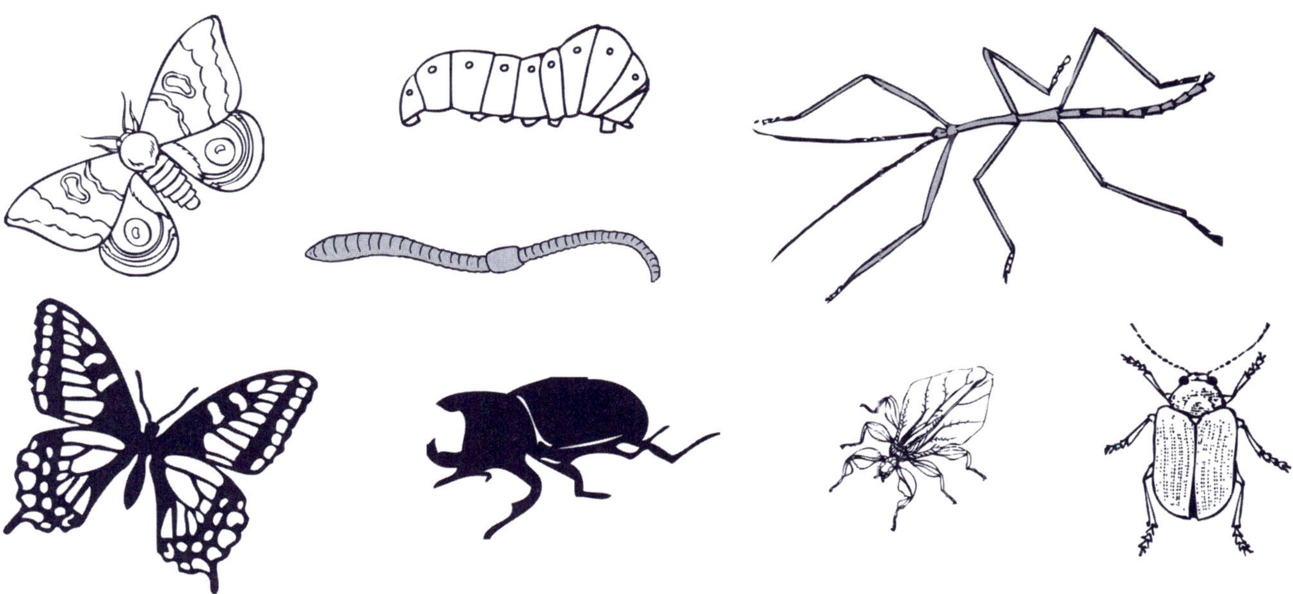

Exercise 9H

Read these words to a friend.
Can you use some of them in sentences?

here	eat	dig	friend
at	big	can	going
boy	girl	as	bed

WEEK 10

Exercise 10A

Say this chant to your friend, pointing to the words.

Insects on icecream **i i i**

Icecream on insects **Delicious!**

Exercise 10B

Fold your paper in half. Draw the sea creatures that live only in the sea on one side and the ones that also go on land on the other side.

Exercise 10C

On your paper, draw the sea creatures in **Exercise 10B** that have tails.

Exercise 10D

On your paper, draw the sea creatures in **Exercise 10B** that have shells.

Exercise 10E

Can you guess what these are? Draw the picture on your paper next to the number.

1 I have fins and a tail.

2 I have a big shell and a small tail.

3 I have nippers.

4 I have big teeth.

5 I have eight legs.

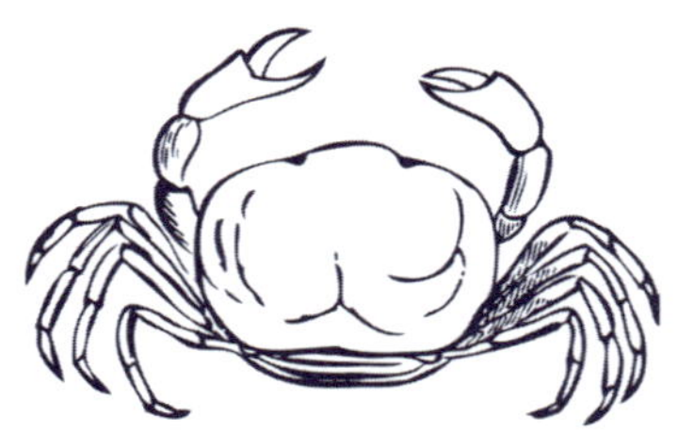

Exercise 10F

Can your fish get home safely? Play this game with a friend.
To play this game you need a dice and two small cardboard fish.

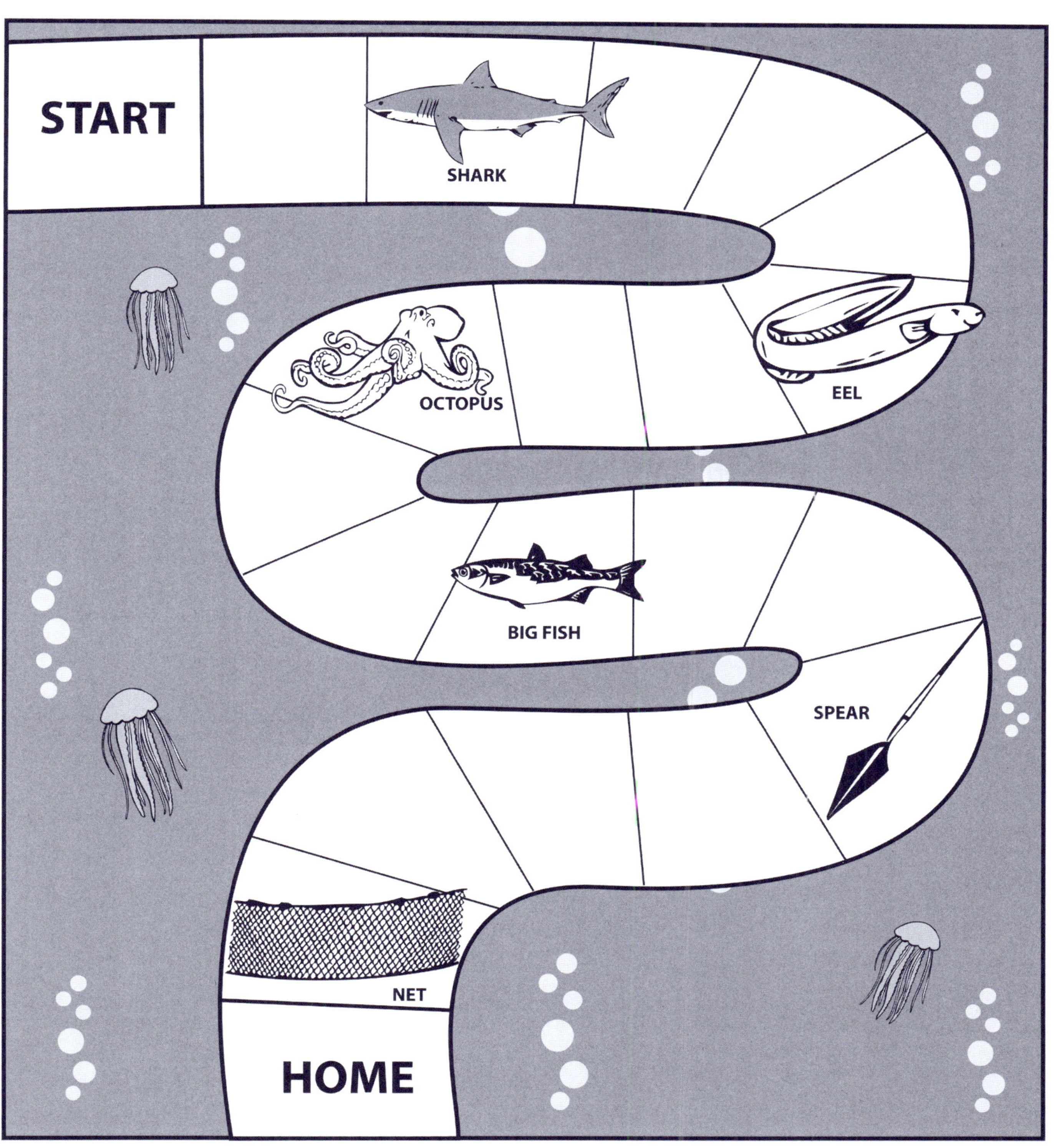

Exercise 10G

Draw all the sea creatures on your paper.

Exercise 10H

Read this story to a friend. Can you find the names of the sea creatures? Draw them.

In the Sea

I see a turtle in the sea.
I see a turtle looking at me.

I see a fish in the sea.
I see a fish looking at me.

I see a jellyfish in the sea.
I see a jellyfish looking at me.

I see an octopus in the sea.
I see an octopus waving at me.

I see a shark in the sea.
Go away shark, don't look at me!

WEEK 1

Exercise 1A

Say this chant to your friend, pointing to the words.

Jellyfish in a jar **j j j**

Jar on a jellyfish **Look at it wriggle!**

Exercise 1B

Say these words and draw the pictures.

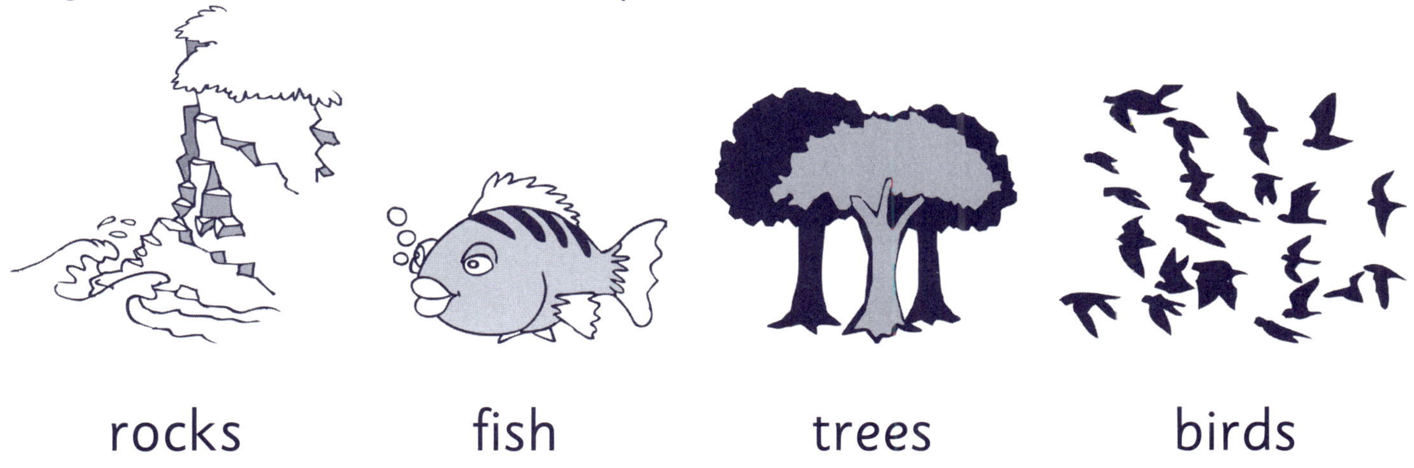

Exercise 1C

Draw all the things you can see in the river.

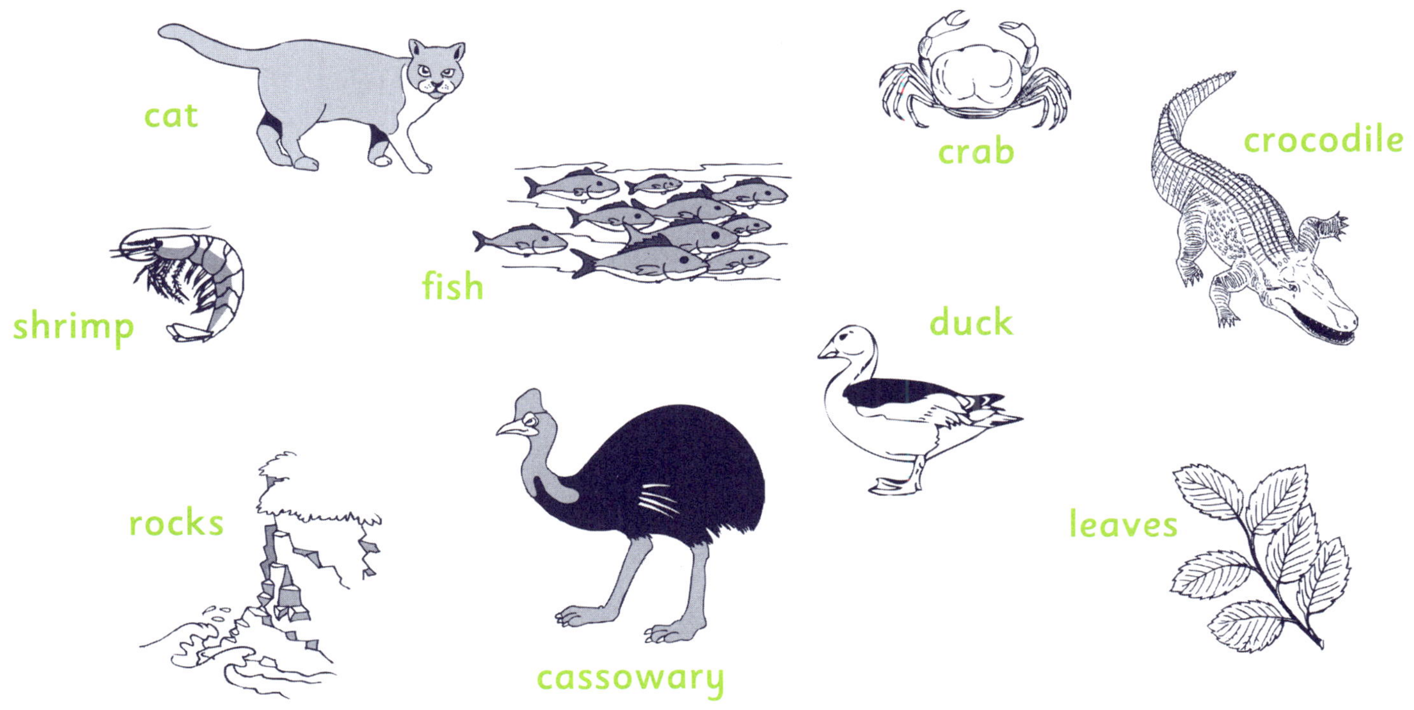

Exercise 1D

Read these sentences to a friend.

We can drink the water in the river.

We can swim in the river.

We can wash our clothes in the river.

We can wash our bodies in the river.

We can go in a canoe on the river.

Exercise 1E

This is a crocodile. Sometimes we call it a croc. Can you draw it?

Exercise 1F

Read this poem to a friend.

I throw rocks, down by the river.
Rocks! Rocks! Rocks!
I see crocs, down by the river.
Crocs! Crocs! Crocs!

Exercise 1G

Say these words to a friend.

it	just	in	jump

WEEK 2

Exercise 2A

Say this chant to your friend, pointing to the words.

Ant on an axe **a a a**
Axe on an ant **Aaaaaah!**

Baby in a bed **b b b**
Bed on a baby **Wah! Wah! Wah!**

Cat on a car **c c c**
Car on a cat **Miaow! Miaow! Miaow!**

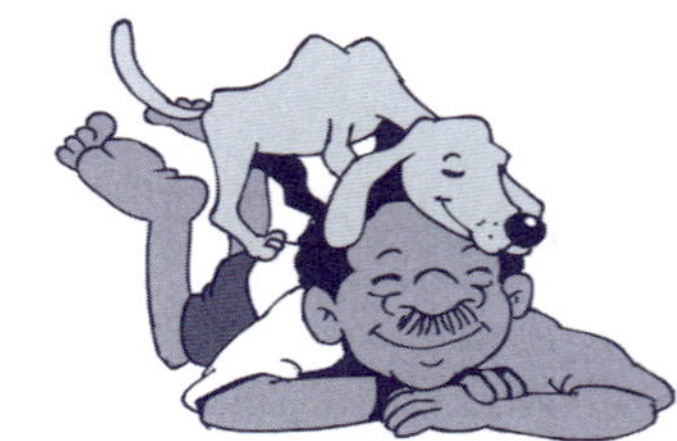

Dog on dad **d d d**
Dad on a dog **Ruf! Ruf! Ruf!**

Eels on eggs **e e e**
Eggs on eels **We're swimming in the water!**

Fly on a fish

Fish on a fly

f f f

Shoo fly, shoo!

Girl on a goat

Goat on a girl

g g g

Get off me!

Hat on a horse

Horse on a hat

h h h

Very very flat!

Insects on icecream

Icecream on insects

i i i

Delicious!

Jellyfish in a jar

Jar on a jellyfish

j j j

Look at it wriggle!

Exercise 2B

Copy these pictures of the moon onto your paper. Put the right name next to each one.

half moon	new moon	full moon

Exercise 2C

Which of these things would you find on the beach? Draw them on your paper.

Exercise 2D

Which of these things can you see in the rock pool when the tide is out? Draw them.

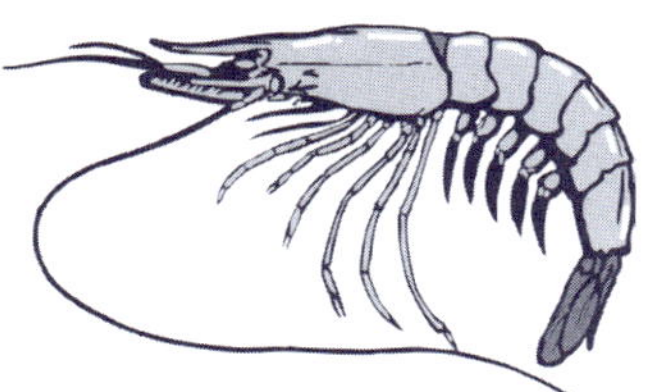

Exercise 2E

Read this story to a friend. Draw the pictures.

I can see the sea. 

I can see the beach. 

I can see shells on the beach. 

I can see rocks on the beach.

I can see a starfish on the beach. 

I can see rubbish on the beach. 

Exercise 2F

Write these letters in your exercise book. Underneath each one, write the words that start with the letter.

b c f i j d

insects	fish	jar	dog	beach	car
in	jump	bed	can	friend	ice
just	fly	dig	cat		

Exercise 2G

Say these words to a friend.

big	come	for	eat
door	an	here	it
can	every	going	is

WEEK 3

Exercise 3A

Say this chant to your friend, pointing to the words.

King on a kite　　k　k　k

Kite on a king　　Ouch!

Exercise 3B

What colour are these things? Draw them on paper and colour them the right colour.

Exercise 3C

This is a yam house that stores yams in the Trobriand Islands. Can you draw it?

Exercise 3D

Draw these things on paper. Colour them with crayons.

a yellow flower

a black fish

a blue bird

a green bug

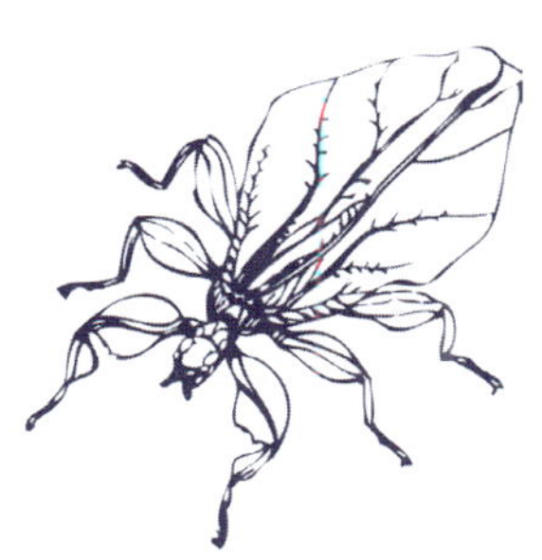

a red flower

Exercise 3E

Tell your friend what is happening in these pictures.

Exercise 3F

Read these words to a friend.

flower	kill	kite	banana
kick	yams	sago	

WEEK 4

Exercise 4A

Say this chant to your friend, pointing to the words.

Leg on a log I I I

Log on a leg **Ouch! Get it off me!**

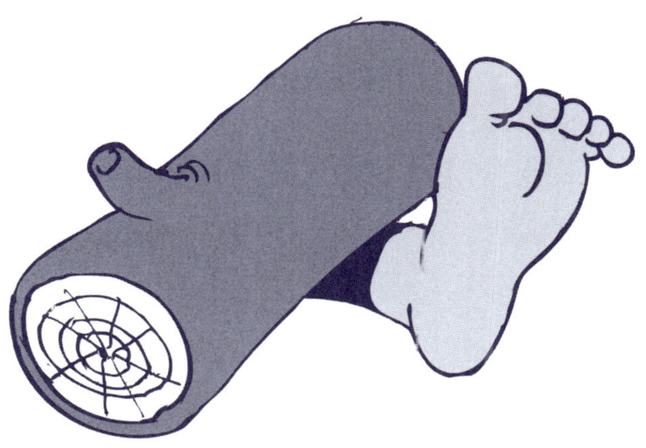

Exercise 4B

Draw the pictures that show bad weather.

Exercise 4C

Read this story to your friend. Draw pictures.

See the trees.

See the wind.

See the rain.

See the sun.

See the landslide.

See the storm.

Exercise 4D

Draw these pictures and match them with the right words. Write the words under your pictures.

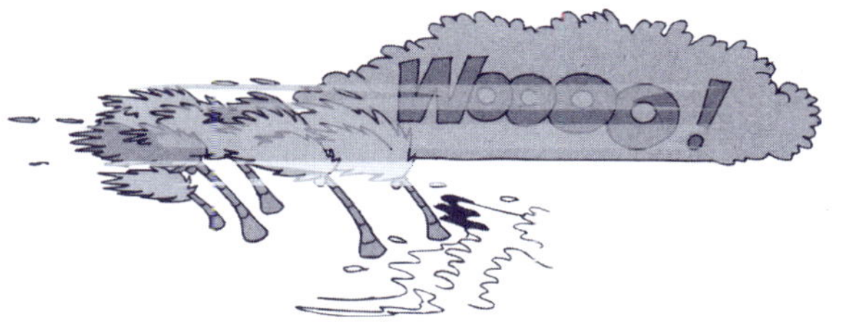

sun	wind	rain

Exercise 4E

What is happening in this comic strip? Tell your friend. Draw it.

Exercise 4F

Write the words that start with **l** in your exercise book.

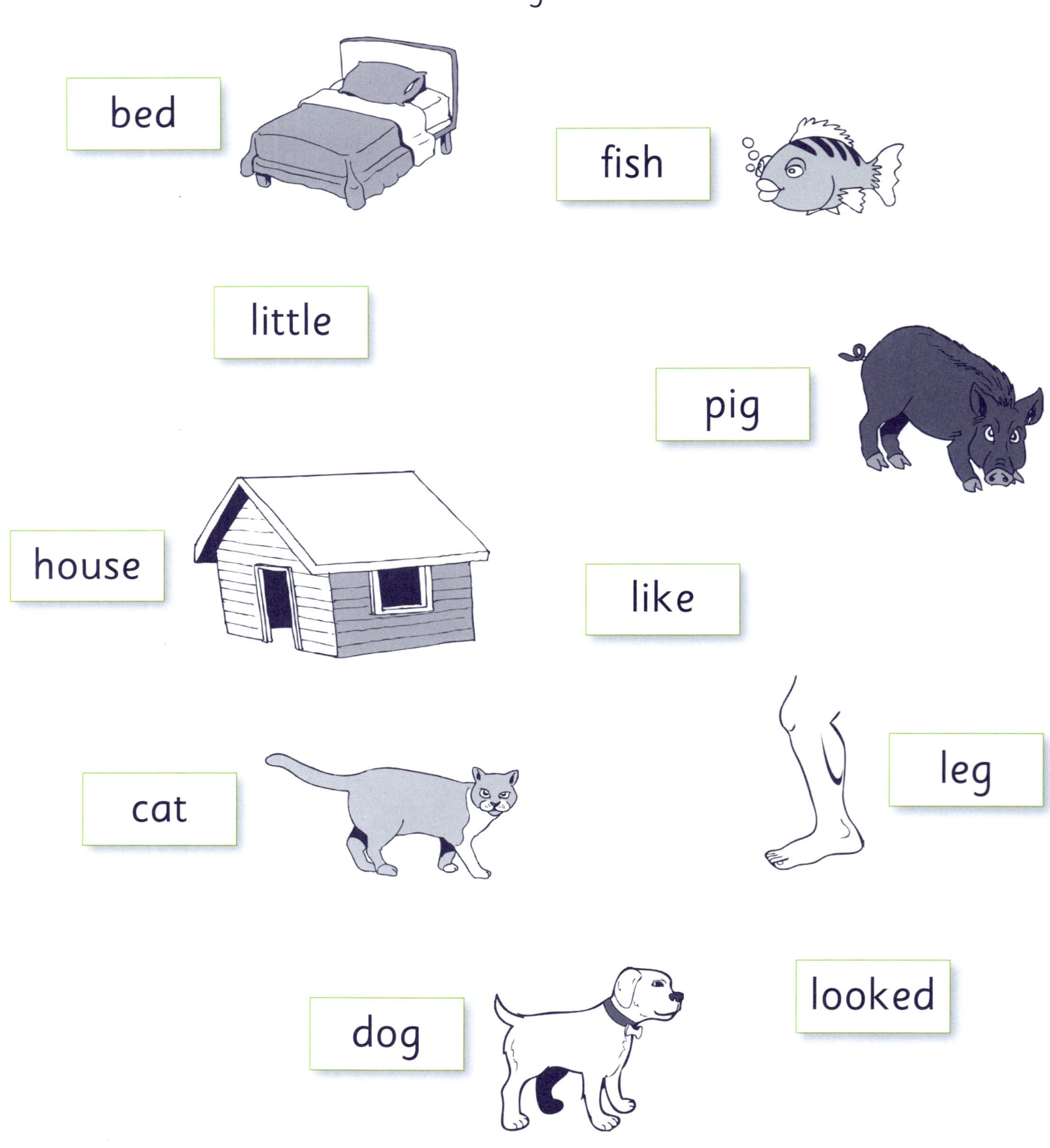

WEEK 5

Exercise 5A

Say this chant to your friend, pointing to the words.

Mat on a mumu m m m

Mumu on a mat Mmmmmmmmmm!

Exercise 5B

What's the weather like today? Draw the picture with the word next to it.

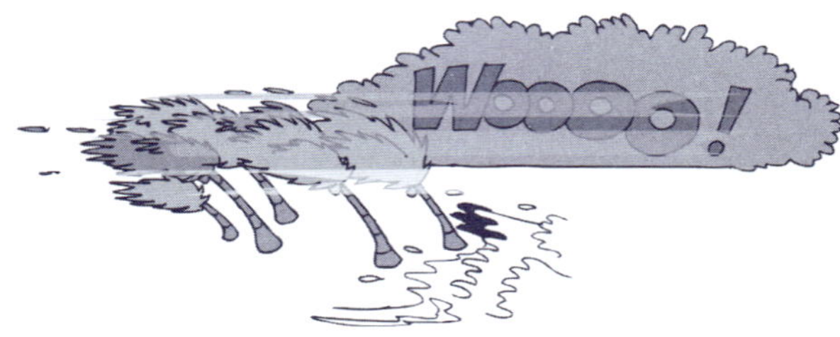

rainy	sunny	stormy

Exercise 5C

Draw these things on your paper and colour them in the right colour.

a red pencil

a blue book

a yellow banana

a red flower

a green leaf

an orange hat

Exercise 5D

On your paper, draw the things you would put in the bin.

Exercise 5E

Read these sentences to a friend.

See the water.

See the reef.

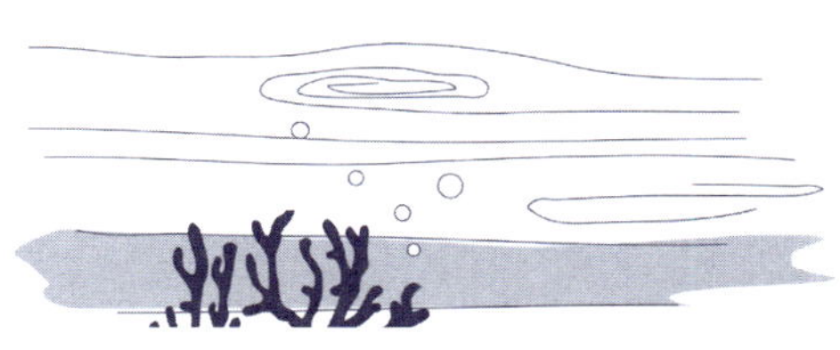

See the coral

underneath.

See the wave

up so high.

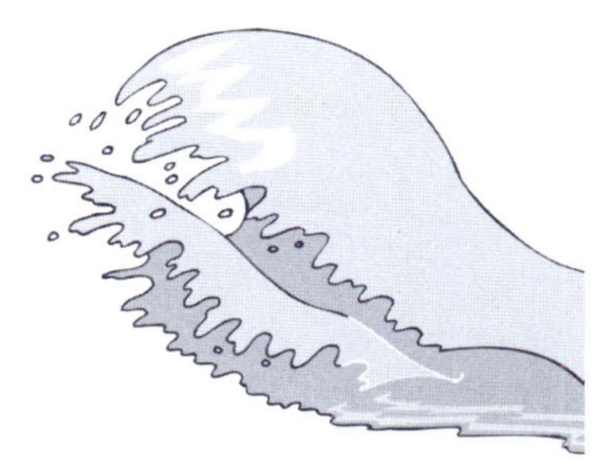

See it go

up to the sky.

Exercise 5F

Find these words in the sentences and then write them in your exercise book.

me	Give me the red book. 
my	This is my friend. 
mum	My mum is here. 

WEEK 6

Exercise 6A

Say this chant to your friend, pointing to the words.

Nuts on a necklace **n n n**

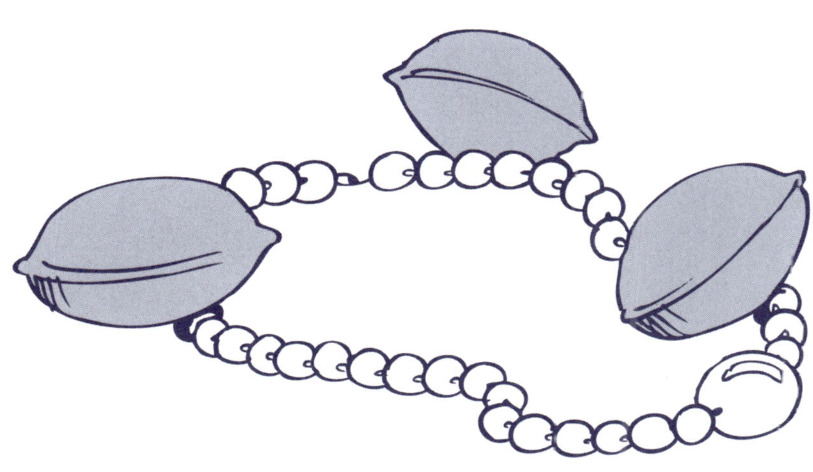

Necklace on nuts **Very pretty!**

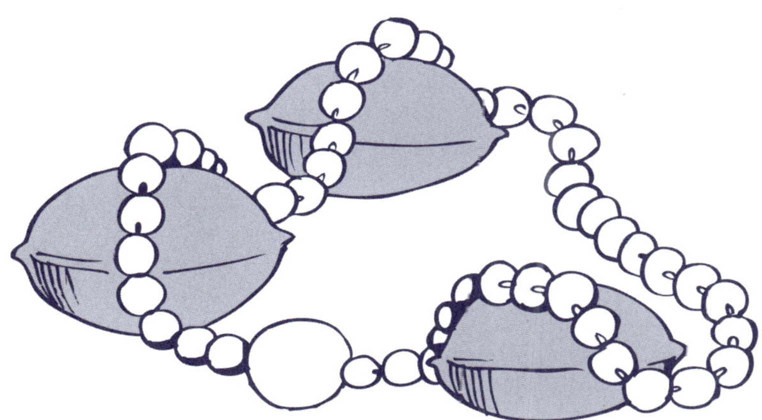

Exercise 6B

Draw these pictures and read the sentences.

The trees are green.

The lava is red.

The volcano is black.

The sky is black.

Exercise 6C

Draw the pictures and write the words next to them.

sun	cyclone	volcano	tsunami

Exercise 6D

Find the same words as the first ones. Write them on your paper. Can you draw a picture for each word?

rain	volcano	sun	rain
sun	tsunami	sun	lava
volcano	name	house	volcano
lava	look	lava	sun

Exercise 6E

On your paper, draw the right picture next to the sentence. Write the number and draw the picture next to it.

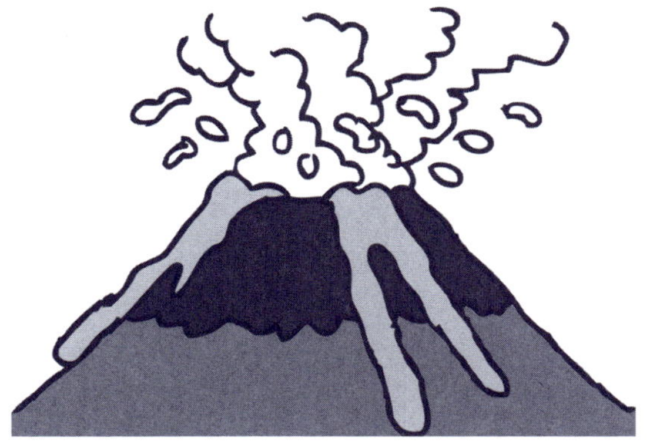

1 See the ash go up in the sky.

2 See the lava go down the volcano.

Exercise 6F

Read these sentences to a friend.

The ground is shaking.

Look at the volcano.

See the red lava.

It is going down the volcano fast.

See the ash go up in the sky.

It is black.

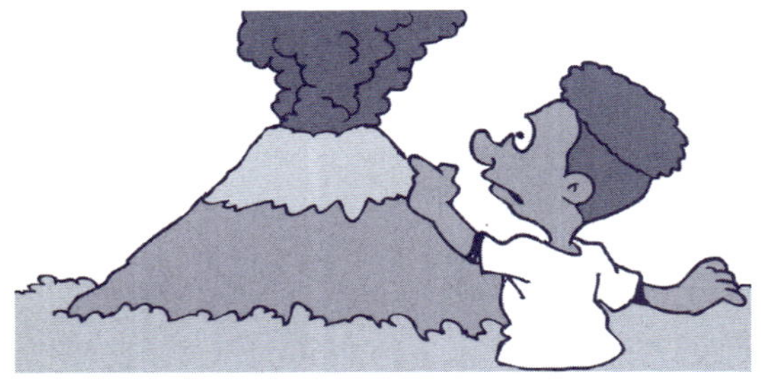

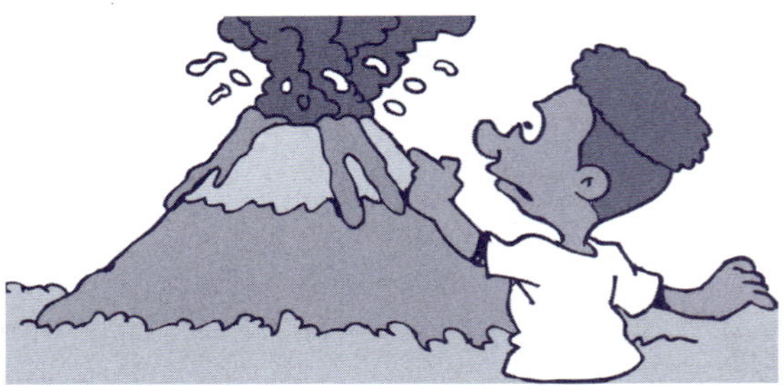

WEEK 7

Exercise 7A

Say this chant to your friend, pointing to the words.

Octopus on an orange **o o o**

Orange on an octopus **See it wriggle!**

Exercise 7B

In your exercise book, write the number that is under each person who could be a brother.

Exercise 7C

Read these sentences to a friend.

This is my brother and my sister.

This is my mother and my sister.

This is my father and my brother.

This is my mother and my father.

Exercise 7D

Match the pictures with the sentences.

My brother can kick the ball.

My sister is small.

Mum is in the house.

Dad is on the truck.

Exercise 7E

Copy this truck. Draw your family on the truck.

WEEK 8

Exercise 8A

Say this chant to your friend, pointing to the words.

King on a kite k k k
Kite on a king Ouch!

Leg on a log l l l
Log on a leg Ouch! Get it off me!

Mat on a mumu m m m
Mumu on a mat Mmmmmmmmm!

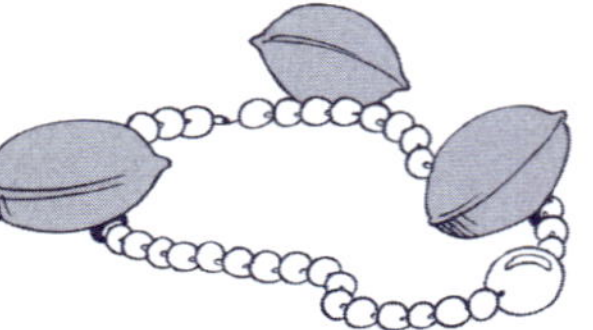

Nuts on a necklace n n n
Necklace on nuts Very pretty!

Octopus on an orange o o o
Orange on an octopus See it wriggle!

Exercise 8B

Find the words that start with the letter in front and write them in your exercise book.

k	leg	kite	mat	kill	orange	boy	he
l	going	come	like	my	just	little	mat
m	me	dig	kick	on	girl	mum	no
n	log	not	looked	no	nuts	play	off

Exercise 8C

Say “Good Morning” or “Good Night” when you point to a picture.

Exercise 8D

Match the names with the pictures.

mother	brother	baby	father	sister

Exercise 8E

Put the letters in each row in alphabetical order.
Write them in your exercise book.

b	d	a	c	e
h	i	g	j	f
k	m	o	l	n

Exercise 8F

Read these sentences to your friend.

This is my dad.
He works in the town.

This is my mum.
She works at the school.

This is my sister Maria.
She helps Mum cook.

This is my brother Ben.
He helps chop wood.

This is me, Pia.
I help to wash the clothes.

WEEK 9

Exercise 9A

Say this chant to your friend, pointing to the words.

Pigs in a pen   p   p   p

Very noisy!   Oink! Oink! Oink!

Exercise 9B

Draw the things we need.

Exercise 9C

Draw the things we don't need.

Exercise 9D

Match the names with the finger puppets.

sister	mother	brother	father

Exercise 9E

Say these words with a friend. Draw the pictures and write the words next to them.

fruit	vegetables	fish	meat	rice

Exercise 9F

Read this story with a friend.

We get food from our gardens.

We get meat from our pigs.

We get meat from our hens.

We get fish from the sea.

We get rice from the shop.

WEEK 10

Exercise 10A

Say this chant to your friend, pointing to the words.

Queen on a quilt   q q q

Quilt on a queen   Go to sleep, your majesty!

Exercise 10B

Draw the traditional clothes.

Exercise 10C

Draw the dolls. Draw the clothes that you wear, on the dolls.

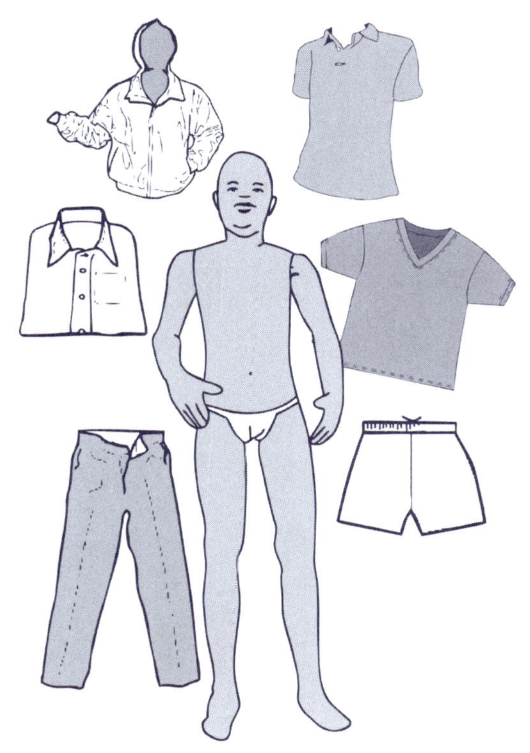

Exercise 10D

Draw all the modern food that we buy in shops.

Exercise 10E

Draw the modern things that you use.

Exercise 10F

Can you read these sentences?

I can go on a truck.

I can go in a canoe.

We cook on a fire.

We cook kaukau.

We cook taro.

We cook yams.

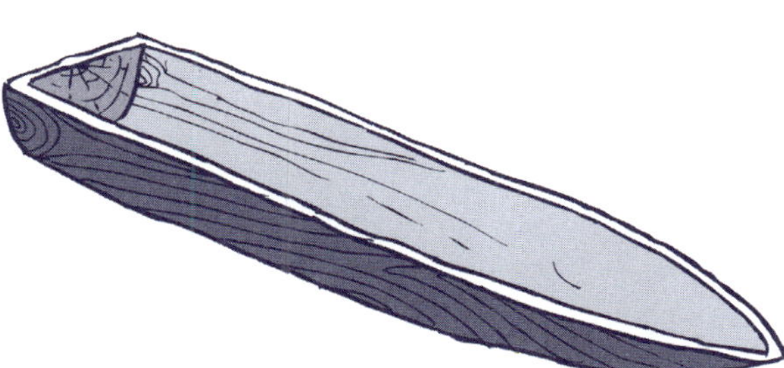

MARKET
SUPERMARKET
BULK STORE
POLICE STATION
POLICE
POLICE

TORE
EMERGENCY
HOSPITAL

WEEK 1

Exercise 1A

Say this chant to your friend, pointing to the words.

Rats on rocks **r r r**

Rocks on rats **Go away rat! Shoo!**

Exercise 1B

Draw the houses that are on the coast.

Exercise 1C

Draw the things that are hunted in your local area.

Exercise 1D

Draw the food that grows in your local area.

Exercise 1E

Read these sentences to your friend.

Ka-ka-ri-ki-ku! Ka-ka-ri-ki-ku!

Wake up father! Wake up mother!

Wake up sister! Wake up brother!

Cock-a-doodle-doo! Cock-a-doodle-doo!

WEEK 2

Exercise 2A

Say this chant to your friend, pointing to the words.

Seagulls on snakes **s s s**

Snakes on seagulls **Sssssssss!**

Exercise 2B

Draw all the buildings on this map and read their names.

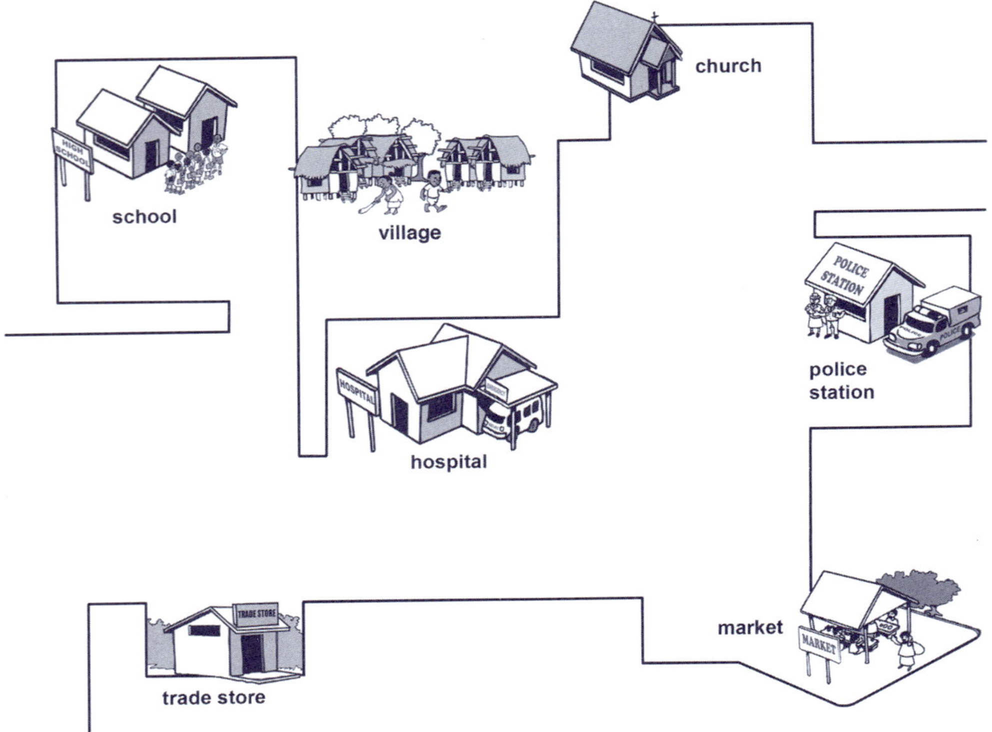

Exercise 2C

Match the place with the person. Draw them next to each other on your paper.

Exercise 2D

Draw these things next to the person who uses them.

Exercise 2E

Fold your paper in half. On one side draw the food that comes from the market and on the other side draw the food that comes from the shops.

Exercise 2F

Read these sentences to a friend.

We go past the trade store.

We go past the church.

We go past the market.

We go past the high school.

We go past the hospital.

We go past the police station.

We go past the children.

Here is our school.

WEEK 3

Exercise 3A

Say this chant to your friend, pointing to the words.

Tail on a turtle   t t t

Turtle on tail   Can you wag your tail?

Exercise 3B

Draw the pictures that go together.

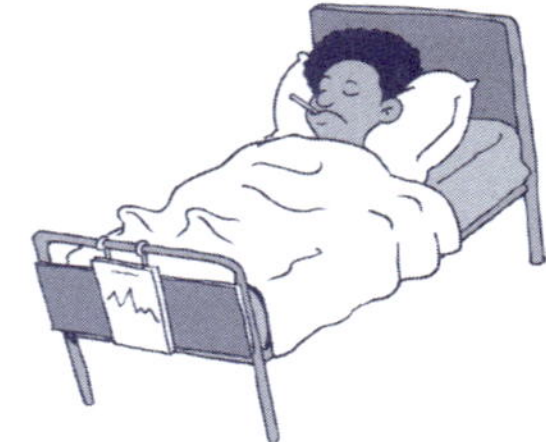

Exercise 3C

Read these sentences. Find these words and say them: **they**, **the**, **this**, **tree**, **to**. Then write them in your exercise book.

Look at the bird in the tree.

They are going to school.

I can go up this tree.

I go to school on the bus.

Exercise 3D

On your paper, draw the person next to the name. Your teacher can help you write these names.

mechanic	doctor	policeman
teacher	nurse	fireman

Exercise 3E

In your exercise book, write the words that start with **t**.

table	icecream	fly
turtle	leg	tree

Exercise 3F

Can you read these sentences to a friend?

We made stick puppets.

We made policemen.

We made teachers.

We made doctors.

We made nurses.

WEEK 4

Exercise 4A

Say this chant to your friend, pointing to the words.

Pigs in a pen p p p
Very noisy! Oink! Oink! Oink!

Queen on a quilt q q q
Quilt on a queen Go to sleep, your majesty!

Rats on rocks r r r
Rocks on rats Go away rat! Shoo!

Seagulls on snakes s s s
Snakes on seagulls Sssssssss!

Tail on a turtle t t t
Turtle on tail Can you wag your tail?

Exercise 4B

Draw the things you like about the market.

Exercise 4C

Draw the things you see for sale at the market.

Exercise 4D

Read this story to a friend.

I am going to the market to buy a big hen. 

I am going to the market to buy a big pig. 

I am going to the market to buy a big pawpaw. 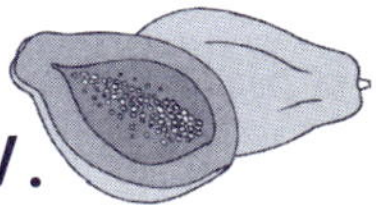

I am going to the market to buy a big yam. 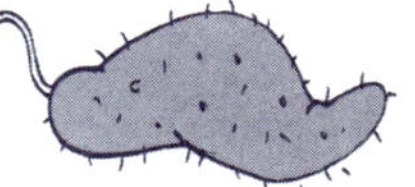

I am going to the market to buy a big fish. 

I am going to the market to buy a big pineapple.

I am going to the market to buy a big taro. 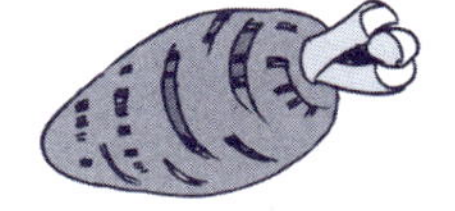

I am going to the market to buy a big banana. 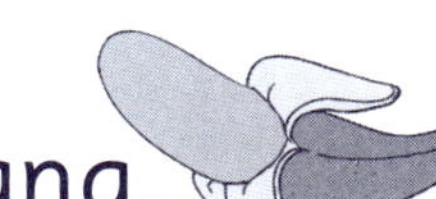 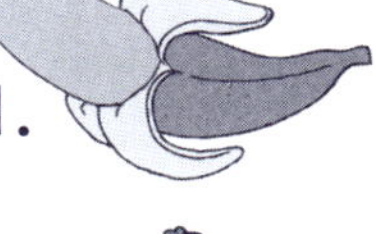

I am going to the market to buy a big laplap. 

For my big wife!

Exercise 4E

Draw this truck. Draw the food that goes to your market on it.
Draw some people too.

Exercise 4F

Write the words that start with the letter in front.

p	pigs	pen	play	leg	put
m	mumu	up	nuts	me	mat
s	snakes	he	she	see	this
t	tail	this	turtle	to	on

WEEK 5

Exercise 5A

Say this chant to your friend, pointing to the words.

Umpire in underpants u u u

Very funny! Ha! Ha! Ha!

Exercise 5B

Fold your paper in half. On one side draw the healthy food and on the other side draw the food that is not healthy.

Exercise 5C

Draw this fruit and colour it in using the correct colours.

Exercise 5D

Look at this menu. Draw all the good food.

Exercise 5E

Read this story to a friend. Draw your favourite picture.

I love icecream, yum yum yum!
I love icecream in my tum.
I love hamburgers, yum yum yum!
I love hamburgers in my tum.

I love hot chips, yum yum yum!
I love hot chips in my tum.
I love sweets, yum yum yum!
I love sweets in my tum.

"Naughty boy!" yelled my mum.
"You won't love your big fat tum!"

Exercise 5F

Read these sentences. Find these words: **up**, **under**, **us**.

Come to school with us.
I am going up on the bus.
Look under the truck.

WEEK 6

Exercise 6A

Say this chant to your friend, pointing to the words.

Van in the village **v v v**

Village in the van **Move over!**
I'm squashed!

Exercise 6B

Draw the way your mum cooks your food.

Exercise 6C

Making a mumu: Draw the food that you put in a mumu.

Exercise 6D

Match the food with the way it is cooked. Draw them next to each other.

Exercise 6E

Look at this shared lunch. Can you read the names of the food?

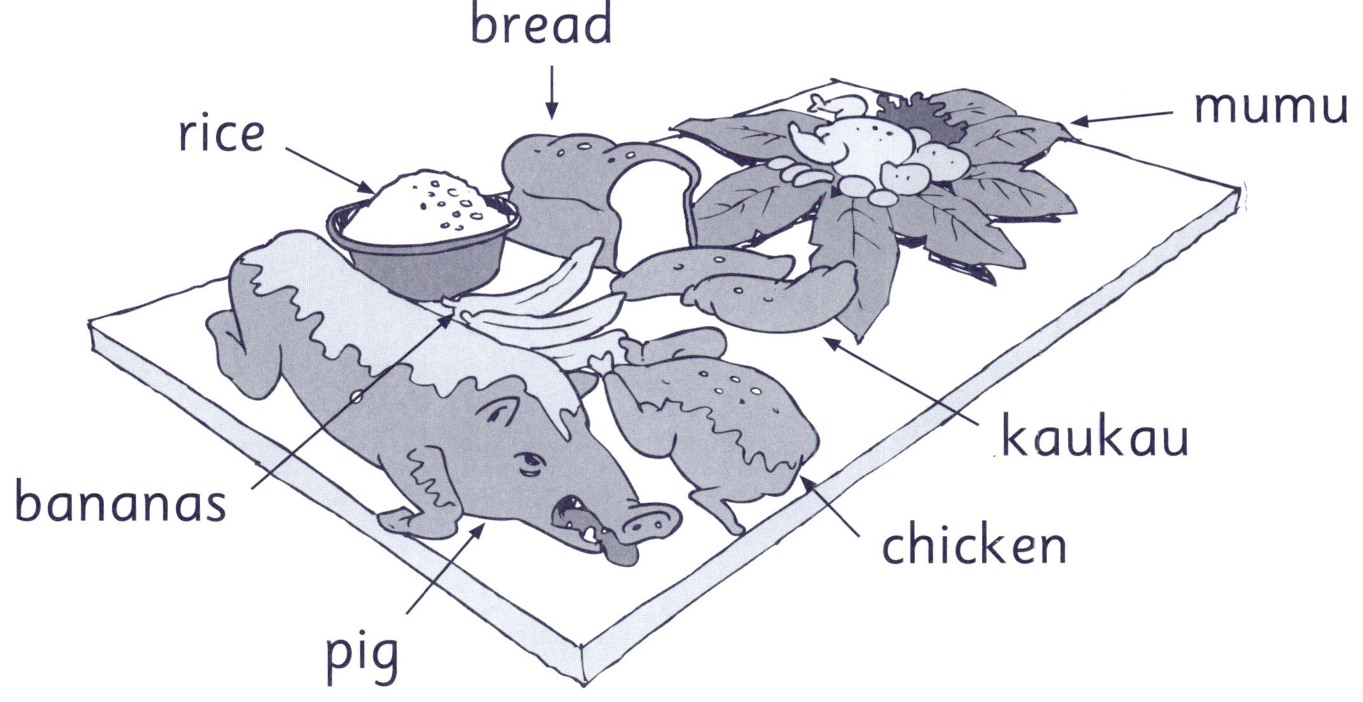

Exercise 6F

Can you write the missing words in your exercise book?

I like m______________.

I like eating r______________.

I like eating b______________ for breakfast.

I like eating p______________.

I like eating b______________.

breadfruit	mangoes	pineapple	bread	rice

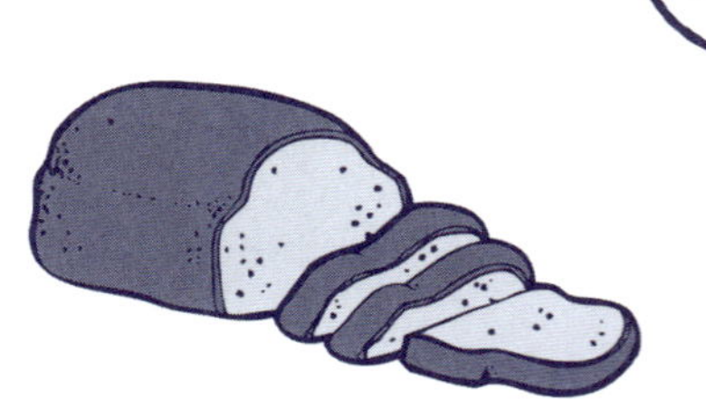

WEEK 7

Exercise 7A

Say this chant to your friend, pointing to the words.

Whale on water **w w w**

Water on whale **Wishy washy water!**

Exercise 7B

What things do we use to keep our body clean and healthy? Draw them on paper.

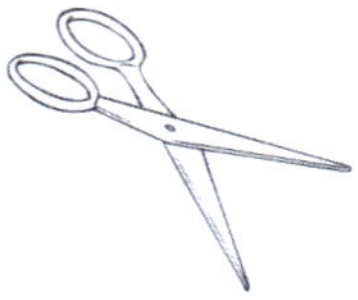

scissors

towel

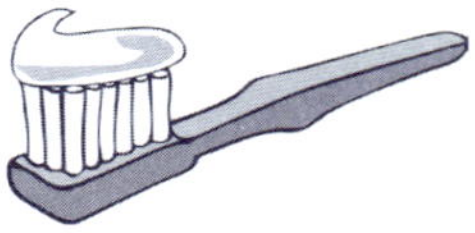

toothbrush

shower

soap

cup

fork

book

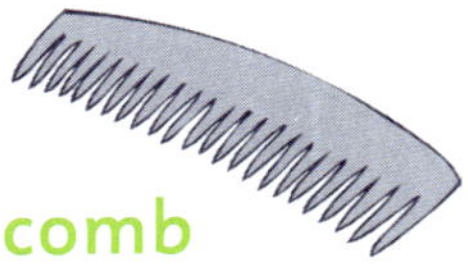

comb

pot

Exercise 7C

Which of the things in **Exercise 7B** do we use to keep our hair clean and healthy?

Draw them on paper.

Exercise 7D

Read these sentences to a friend.

I wash my hands.

I make bubbles.

I wash my hair.

I make big bubbles.

I clean my teeth.

I make small bubbles.

I wash my face.

I make nose bubbles.

Ha! Ha! Ha!

Exercise 7E

Find the words to go in the spaces. Write them in your exercise book.

We use s________________ to cut hair.

We use s________________ to wash our hands.

We use a t________________ to dry our hands.

We use a c________________ to comb our hair.

We use a t________________ to clean our teeth.

toothbrush	comb	scissors	soap	towel

Exercise 7F

Match the things below with the things above. Draw them together.

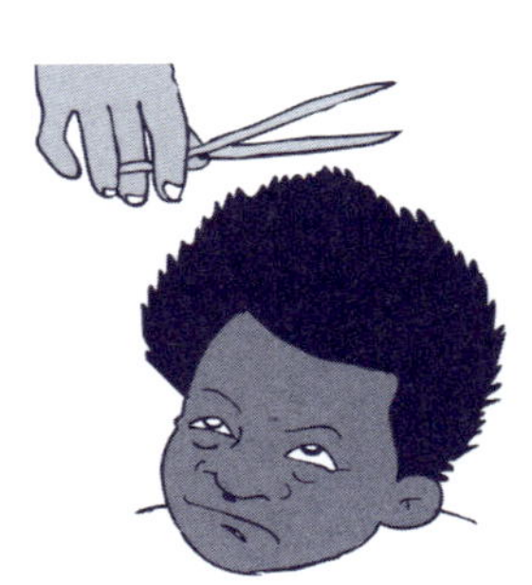

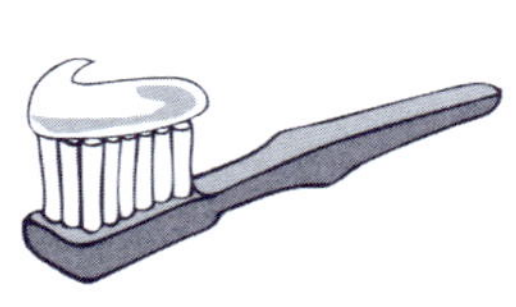
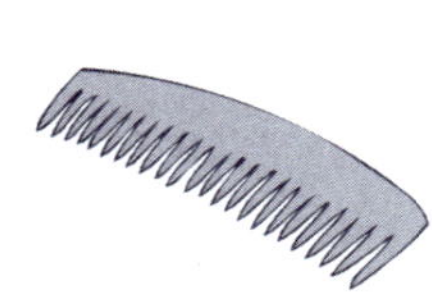

WEEK 8

Exercise 8A

Say this chant to your friend, pointing to the words.

Box on ox **x x x**

Ox on box **I'm the king of the castle!**

Exercise 8B

Match the sentences with the pictures. Draw each picture on your paper and say the sentence.

I'm washing the floor.

Mum is putting the rubbish in the bin.

I'm washing the dishes.

I'm sweeping the floor.

Mum is washing the clothes.

Exercise 8C

Choose the words to go in the spaces. Write them in your exercise book.

I'm sweeping the f_______________.

I'm cleaning the w_______________.

I'm shaking the m_______________.

I'm washing the d_______________.

I'm putting rubbish in the b_______________.

bin	window	mat	floor	dishes

Exercise 8D

Draw this bin. Find the rubbish and draw it in the bin.

Exercise 8E

What's in the box? Draw the box and write the name next to it.

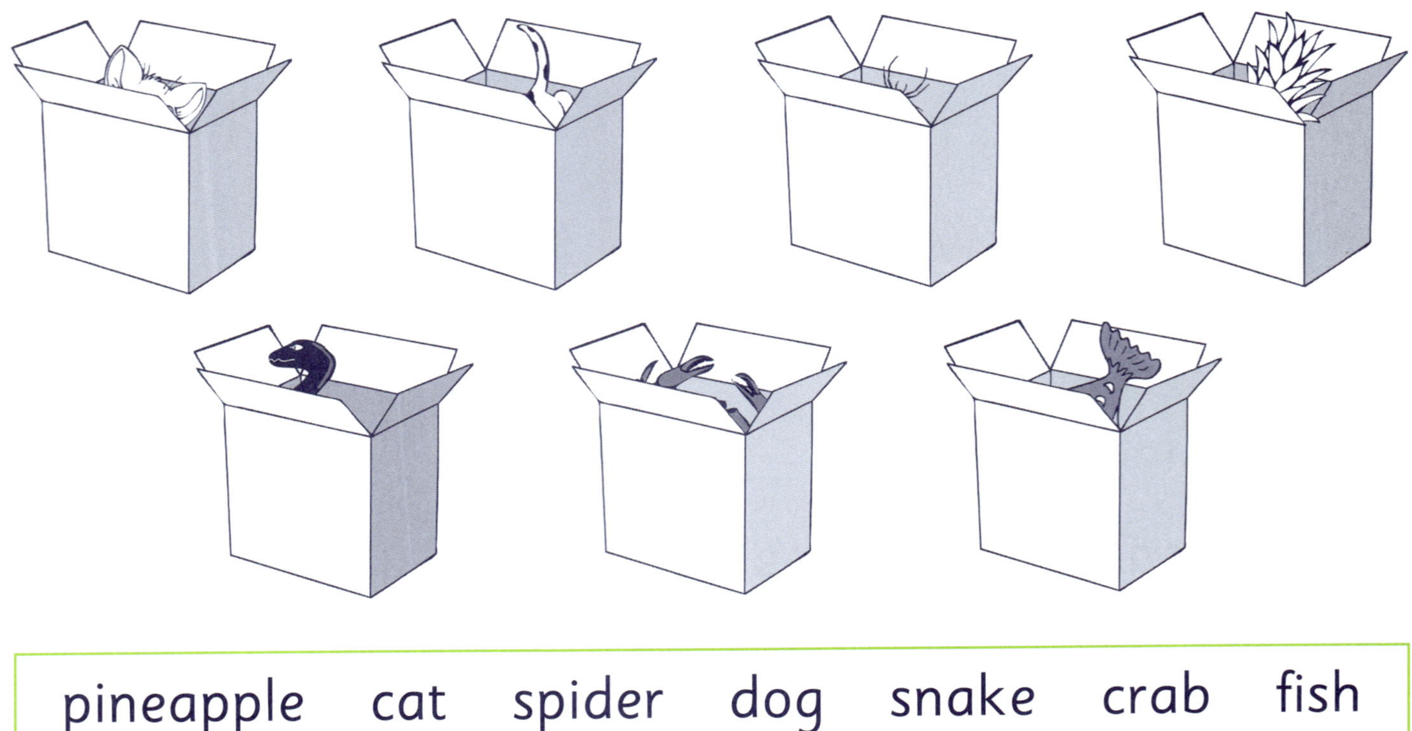

pineapple cat spider dog snake crab fish

Exercise 8F

Write these words in your exercise book and circle the **x**.

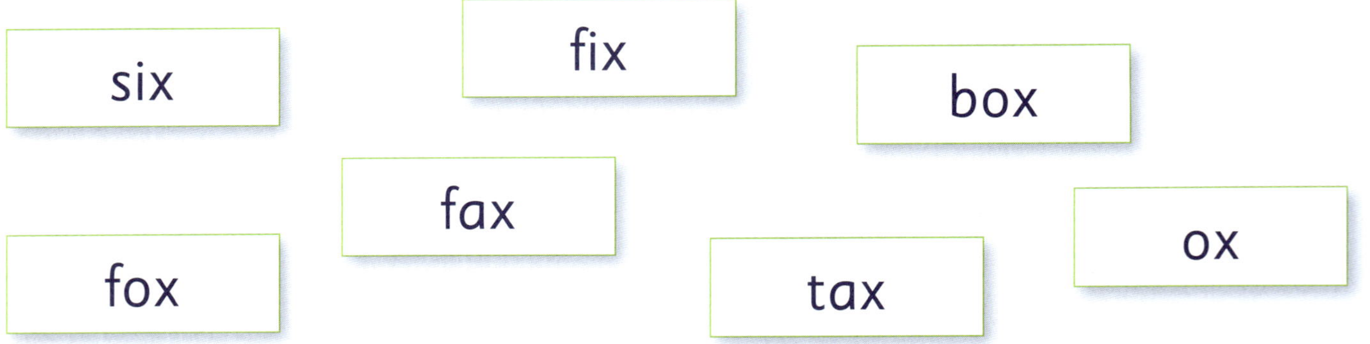

six fix box fax fox tax ox

WEEK 9

Exercise 9A

Say this chant to your friend, pointing to the words.

Yams in a yard y y y

Very yummy! **Yum! Yum! Yum!**

Exercise 9B

Draw the truck with the cargo on it that starts with **y**.
Write the word underneath.

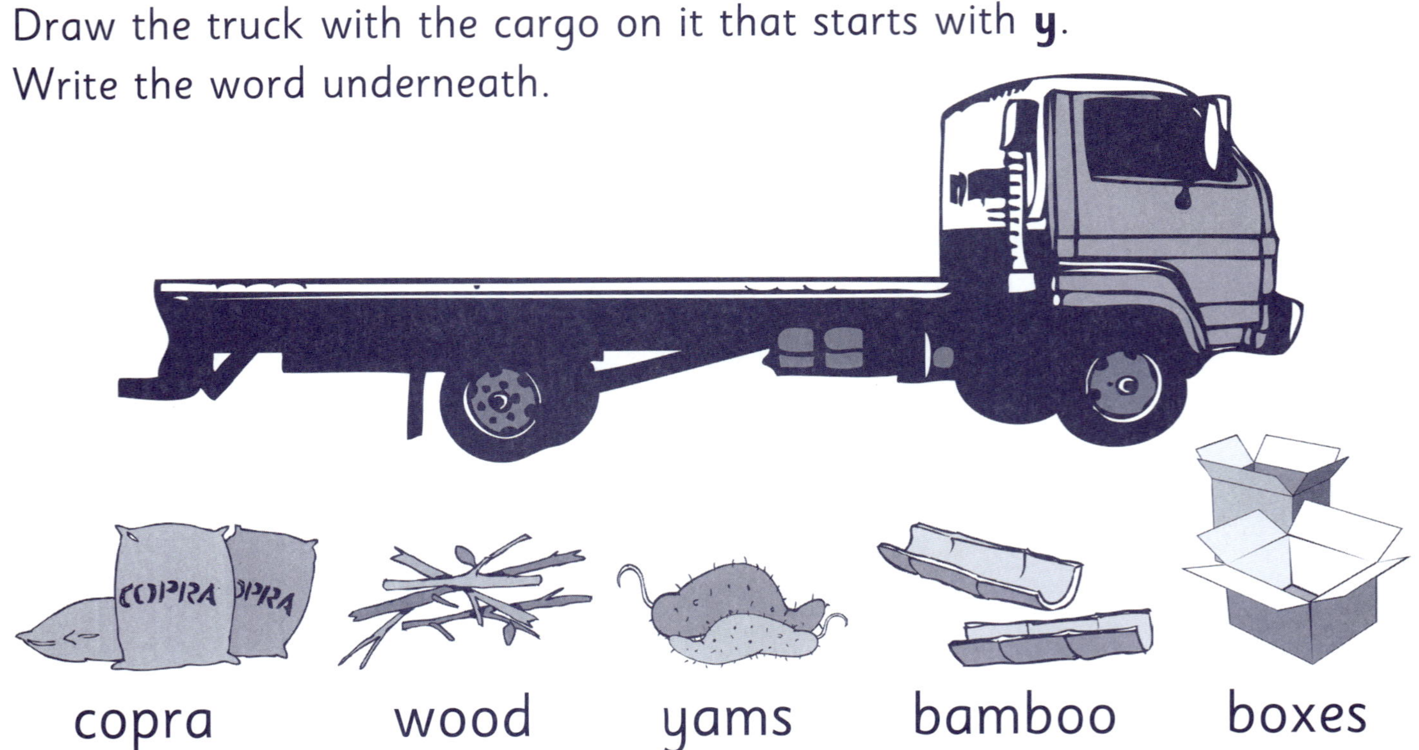

Exercise 9C

Draw the things that go fast.

Exercise 9D

Draw the bus. Draw your family on the bus.

Exercise 9E

Read these sentences to a friend.

My truck is red.

My truck goes fast.

My bus is going to town.

My bus is going to school.

My truck is going to the market.

My truck is going to the village.

Exercise 9F

Put in the missing letters.

v	w	x	y

bo__   __ater   __ams   __an

WEEK 10

Exercise 10A

Say this chant to your friend, pointing to the words.

Zip on Zorro z z z

See his sword go ... Zip! Zap! Zing!

Exercise 10B

Draw the boat that goes slow.

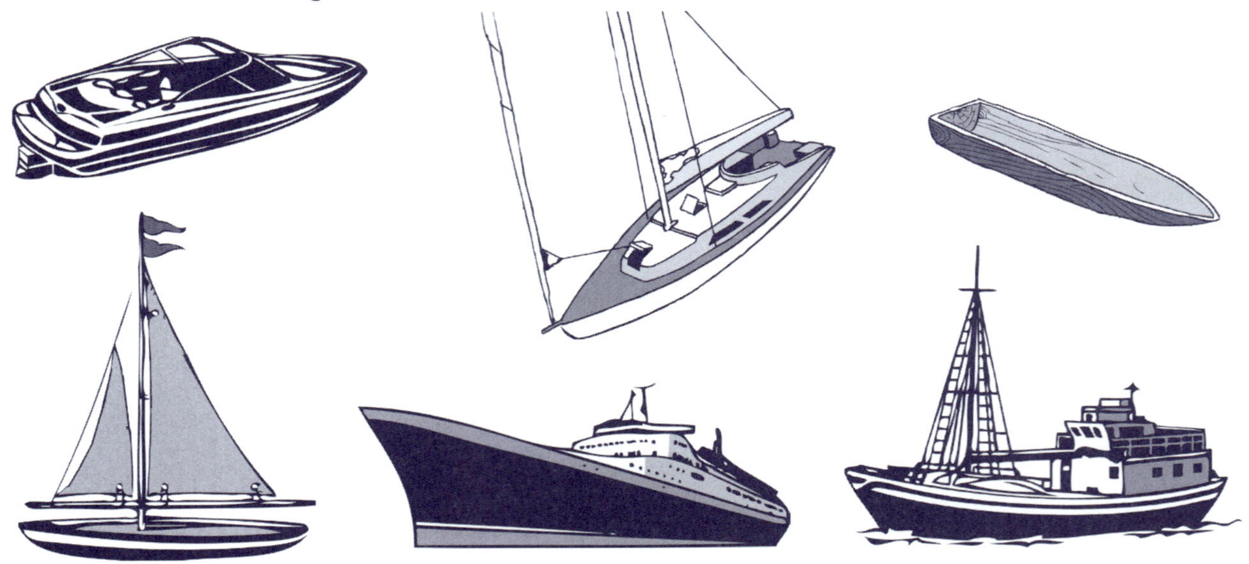

Exercise 10C

Write the correct word for each picture and draw it. Then say each one.

plane	boat	ship	canoe	bus	truck

Exercise 10D

Draw the plane that flies to Australia.

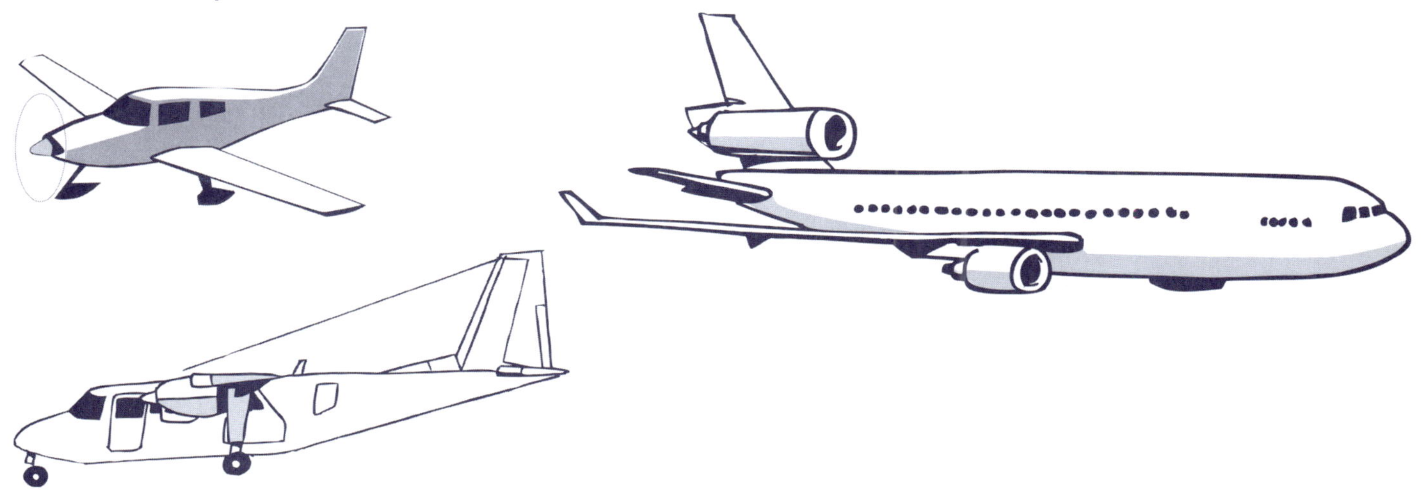

Exercise 10E

Match the sentence with the picture. Say the sentence and point to the correct picture with your friend.

See the people on the ship.

See the plane go up.

See the boxes on the ship.

See the plane go down.

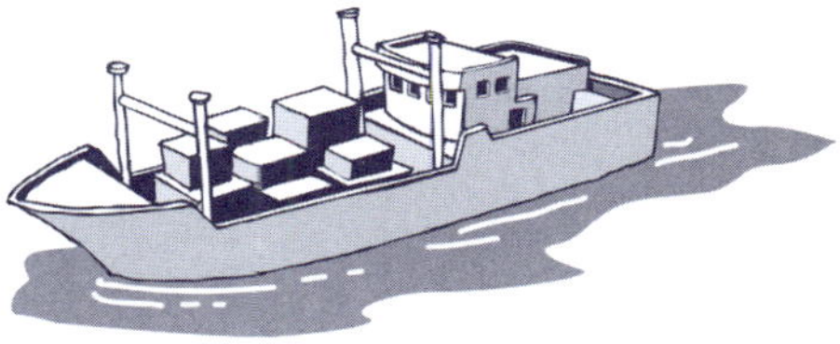

WEEK 1

Exercise 1A

Put these letters in alphabetical order.

d f e a c b

Exercise 1B

Put your flowers and leaves in these patterns, or draw them.
Point to each picture and say **flower** or **leaf**.

Exercise 1C

Put your seeds and shells (or stones) in these patterns, or draw them.

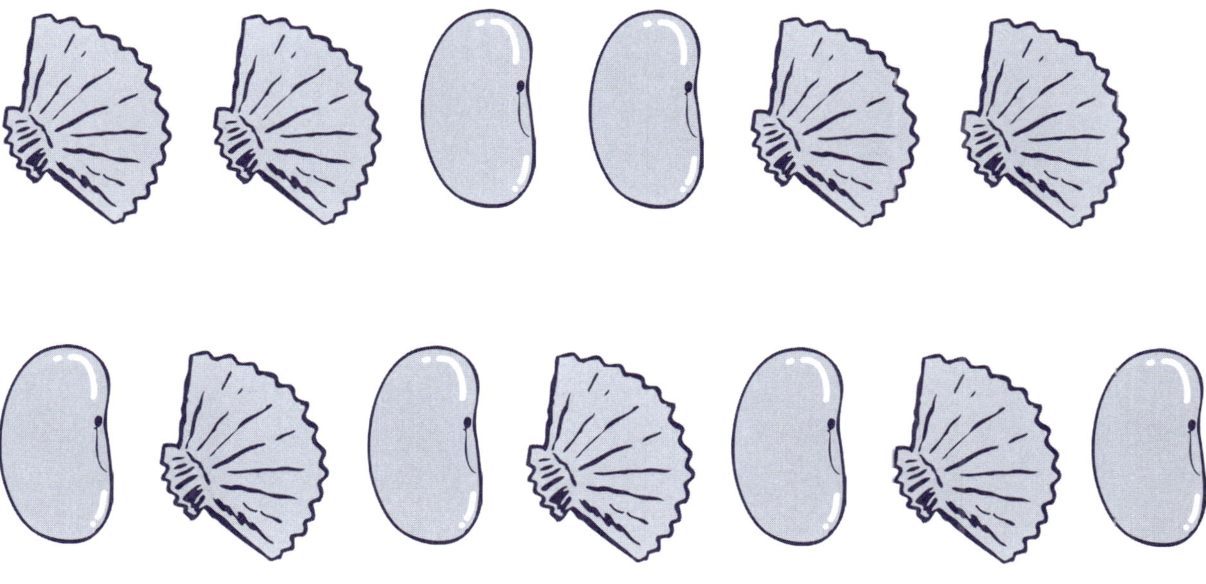

Exercise 1D

Draw the long necklace with flowers and leaves on your paper.

Exercise 1E

On a piece of paper, draw a child doing these things.

walk

hop

jump

run

Exercise 1F

Read these sentences to a friend.

I am jumping, jumping, jumping,
I am jumping like a cricket.

I am flying, flying, flying,
I am flying like a bird.

I am hopping, hopping, hopping,
I am hopping like a frog.

WEEK 2

Exercise 2A

Put these letters in alphabetical order.

f e h d g

Exercise 2B

Can you make these word ladders? Write them in your exercise book and finish the words. Say them to a friend.

can	cat
___an	___at
___an	___at
___an	___at
___an	___at
___an	___at
___an	___at
___an	___at

b r v f s t m p h

Exercise 2C

Can you copy these patterns? Draw them on paper.

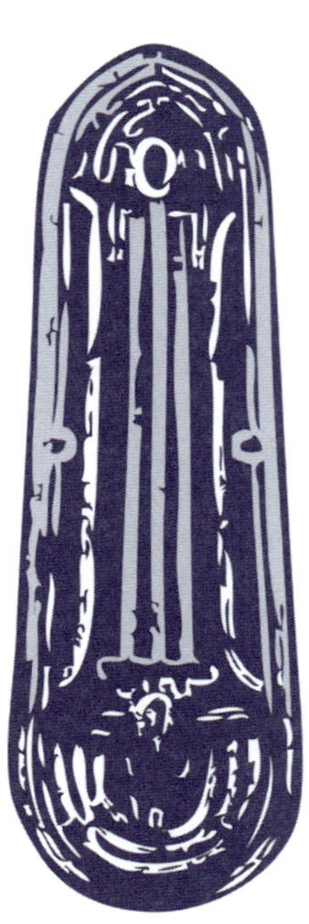

Exercise 2D

Look at these headdresses. Copy the one you like the best onto your paper.

Exercise 2E

Read these sentences to your friend. Draw the truck.

Dad got a new truck.

It was big and red.

He liked his truck.

"Can I come for a ride?" said Ben.

"Can I come too?" said Pia.

"Can I come too?" said Maria.

"Can I come too?" said Mum.

"Can I come too?" said Grandma.

"Can I come too?" said Grandpa.

"Yes," said Dad. "Get in!"

Exercise 2F

Draw these things on your paper.

an armband	a kina shell	a headdress

WEEK 3

Exercise 3A

Put these letters in alphabetical order.

k i l j

Exercise 3B

Can you make words with these letters and the sound in the circle? Write them in your exercise book.

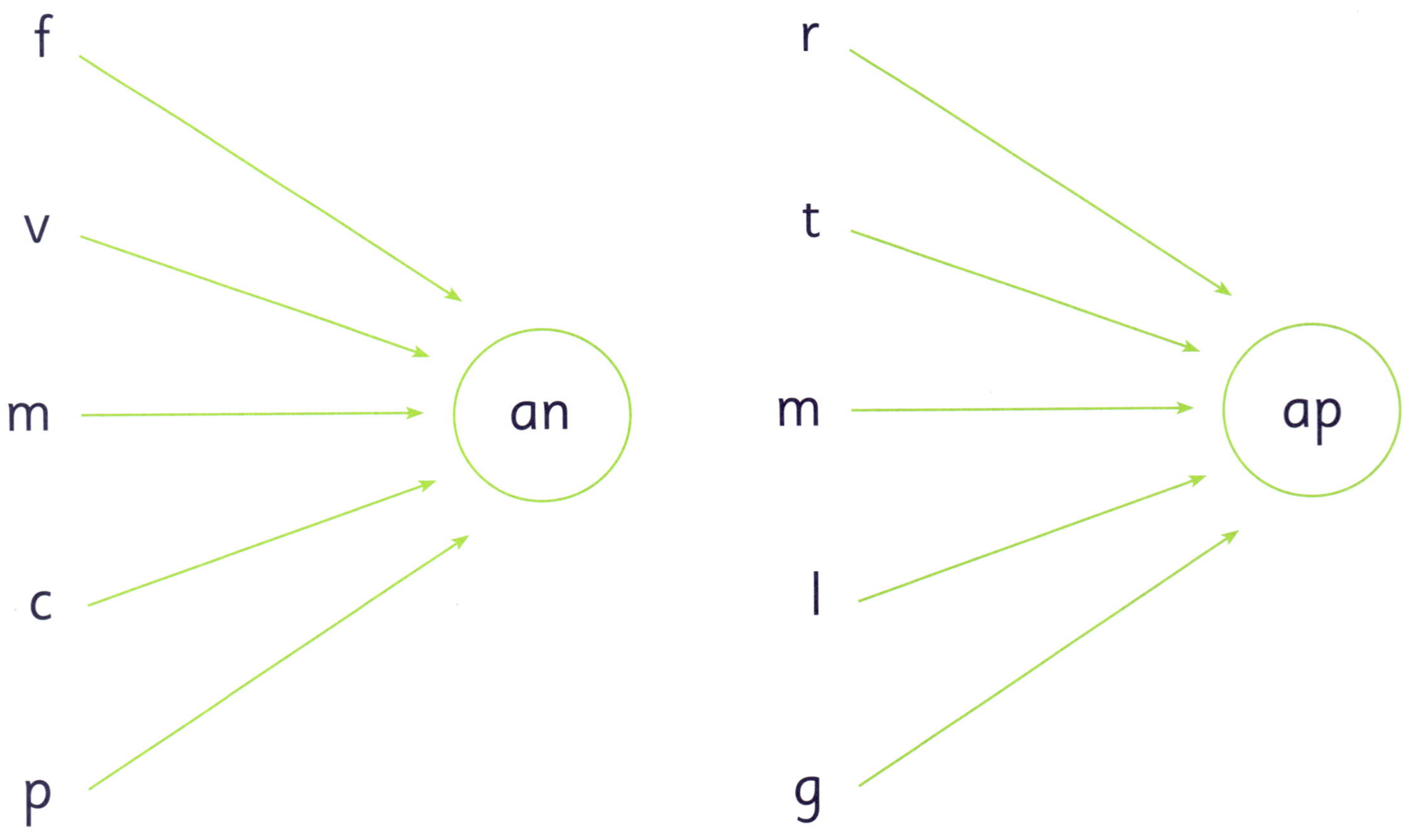

Exercise 3C

Put in the missing words. Look at the pictures first.

We	I	You

Exercise 3D

Read this to a friend.

We can clap.

We can jump.

We can sing.

We can tap.

We can dance.

We can rap.

We can hip hop.

Exercise 3E

Match the pictures with the sentences.

Draw and write them in your exercise book.

We can dance.	We can sing.	We can clap.

WEEK 4

Exercise 4A

Put these letters in alphabetical order.

o p n m

Exercise 4B

Look at this boy. Draw him on paper.
Say the parts of his body to a friend.

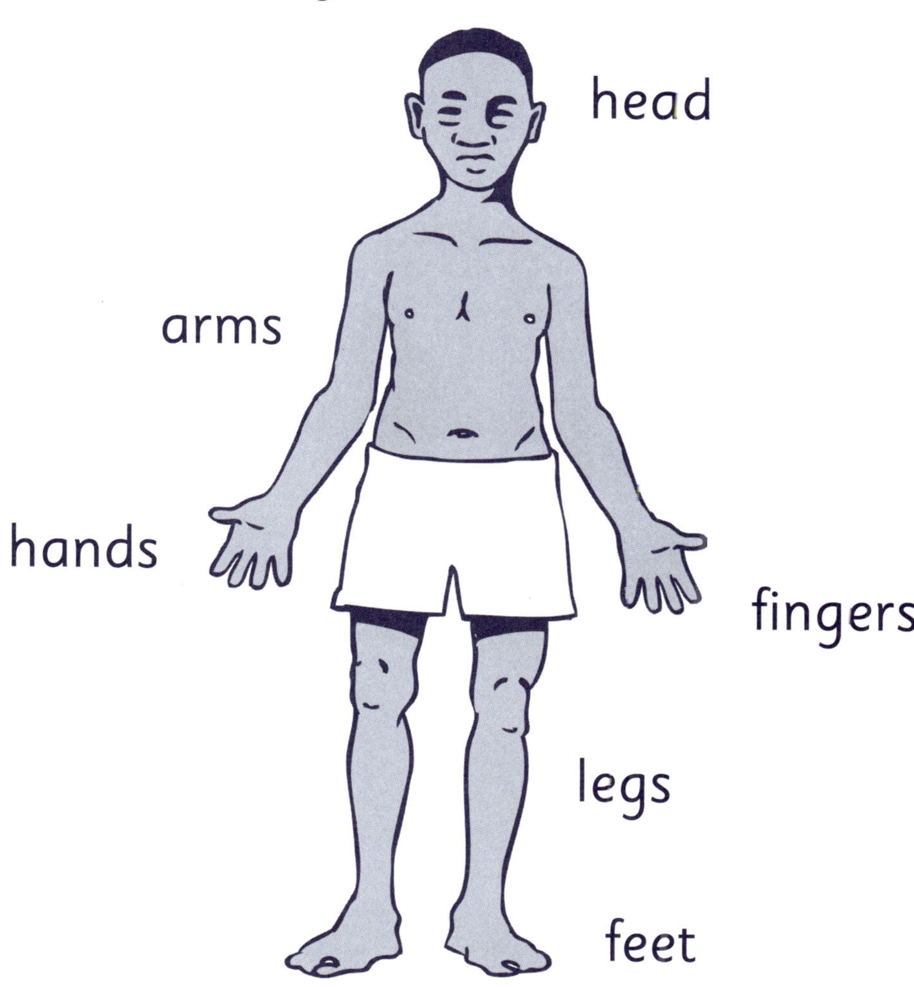

Exercise 4C

Can you say these words to a friend?

Pam	ham	yam	ram
dam	Sam	tab	dab
jab	cab	nab	

Exercise 4D

Can you read these sentences? Can you do them?

I can clap my hands.

I can stamp my feet.

I can snap my fingers.

I can wave my arms.

I can slap my legs.

I can nod my head.

Exercise 4E

Can you find the correct word? Read these to a friend.

I am __________. 	I am __________. 	I am __________. 
I am __________. 	I am __________. 	I am __________. 

dancing	jumping	singing
hopping	clapping	stamping

Exercise 4F

Read this story to a friend.

Simon says, "Shut the window!"

Simon says, "Shut the door!"

Simon says, "Go to the table!"

Simon says, "Run to the garden!"

Simon says, "Give me the red pencil!"

Simon says, "Put the book in the box!"

Simon says, "Clap your hands!"

Simon says, "Jump up and down!"

Simon says, "Give me your lunch!"

John says, "No way!"

WEEK 5

Exercise 5A

Put these letters in alphabetical order. Start with **q**.

s u t q r

Exercise 5B

Look at these pictures. Draw them on your paper and colour them in these colours.

a red nose

blue eyes

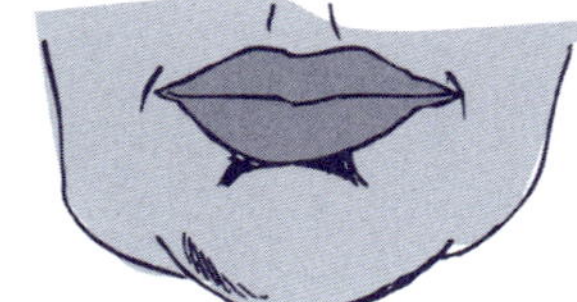

a white chin

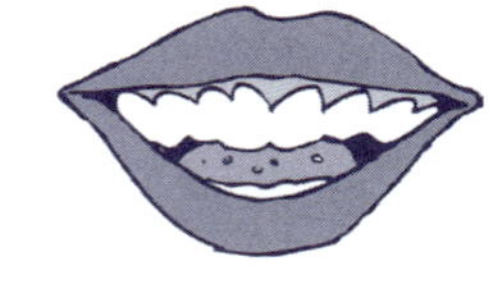

a black mouth

Exercise 5C

Draw the pictures and write the correct word below each picture.

pen	hen	men	ten

Exercise 5D

Can you climb this coconut tree to get the coconut? You must say all the words.

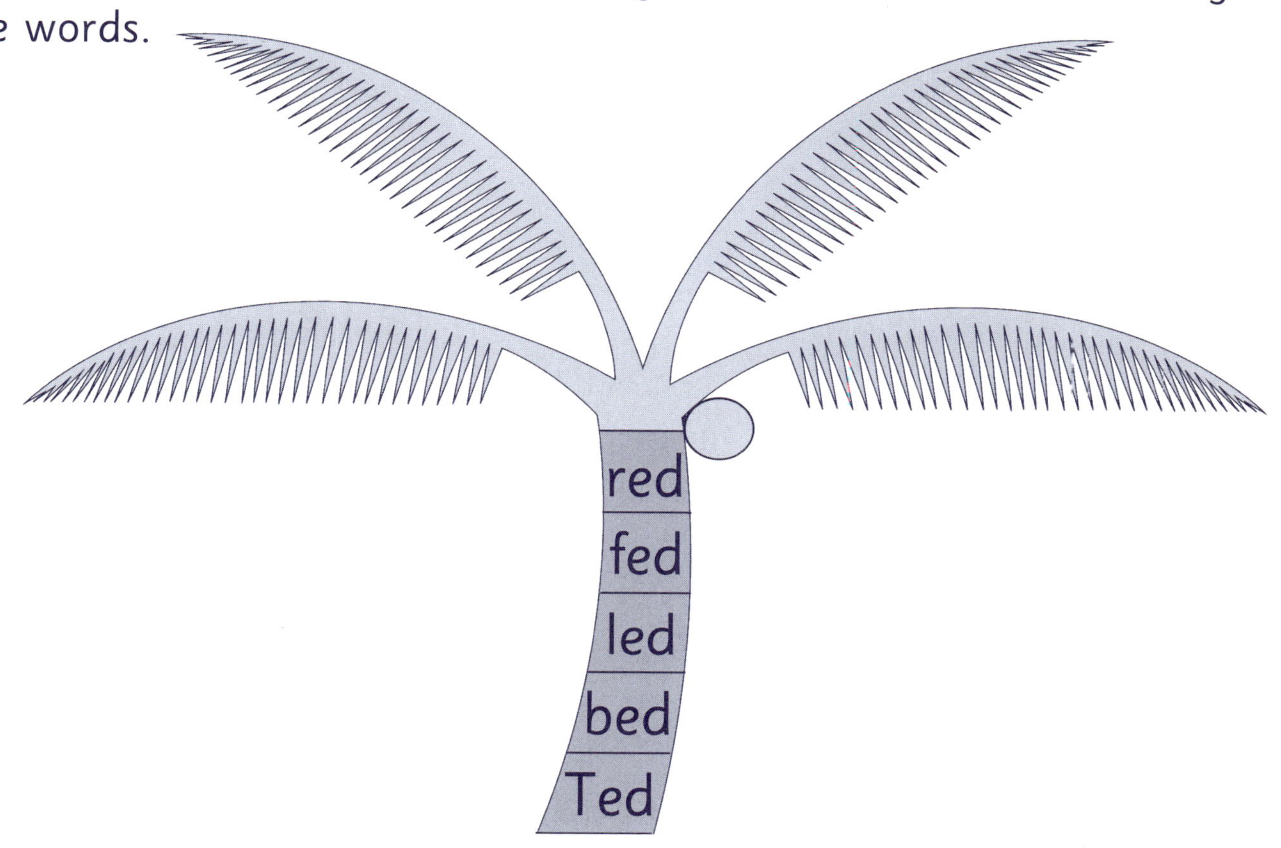

Exercise 5E

Write the beginning letter for each picture in your exercise book.

Exercise 5F

Look at this face. Draw it on your paper and colour it in with these colours.

Exercise 5G

Describe these people's faces to a friend.

WEEK 6

Exercise 6A

Put these letters in alphabetical order. Start with **u**.

v u x w

Exercise 6B

Where do these words belong? Make the boxes in your exercise book and write in the correct words. Then say them.

ed	en	et	eg

Exercise 6C

Look at this traditional art. Can you draw some of these things? Do you know what they are? Tell your friend.

Exercise 6D

Can you read these sentences to a friend?

Look at the wet fishing net.

We can get a pet.

See the jet go up.

Exercise 6E

Look at the pictures and draw them. Write the correct sentence under each picture.

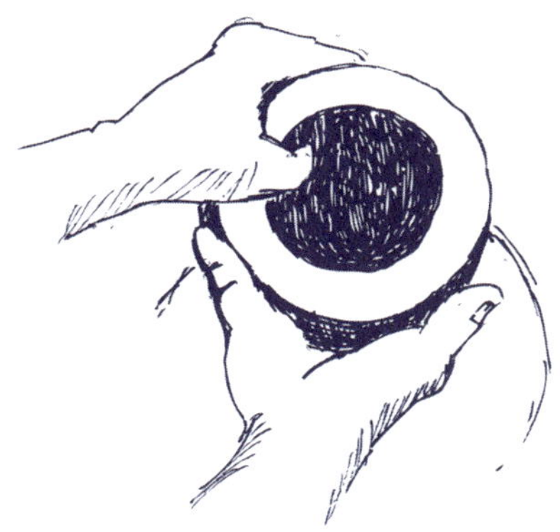

We made grass skirts.

We made clay masks.

We made clay pots.

WEEK 7

Exercise 7A

Put these words in alphabetical order. Look at the first letter.

cat ant dog eggs baby

Exercise 7B

Where do these words belong? Make these boxes in your exercise book and write in the correct words. Then say them.

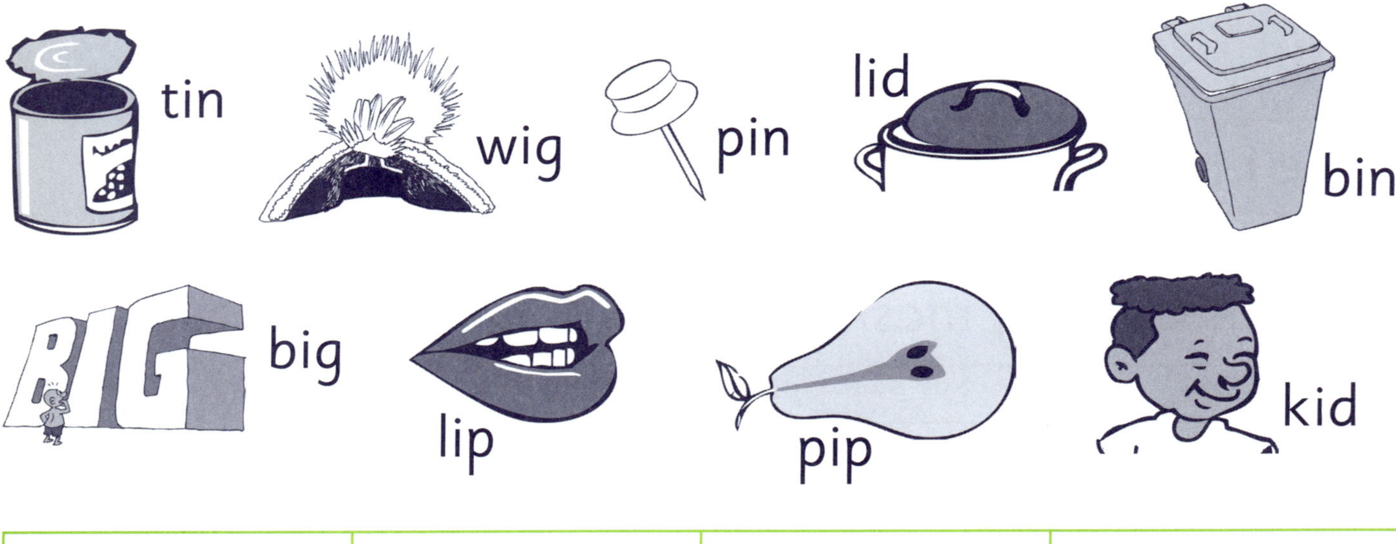

ig	ip	id	in

Exercise 7C

Look at this traditional art. Do you know what each one is? Choose one to draw and write the correct sentence under your picture.

We made clay pots.

We made masks.

We made shields.

We made tapa cloth.

We made a crocodile head.

Exercise 7D

Can you read these sentences to a friend?

The pig can dig a big hole.

Put the fish fin in the bin.

The kid put the lid on the jar.

Exercise 7E

Can you climb up this word ladder? Say all the words.

pig
big
wig
rig
dig
fig
jig

Exercise 7F

Draw the bus driver on your paper. His name has **am** in it. Write his name.

WEEK 8

Exercise 8A

Put these words in alphabetical order. Look at the first letter.

fish mat rocks jellyfish kite leg

Exercise 8B

On your paper, draw all the things that have **in** in them.

Exercise 8C

Say these words, then match them with the same sounds.

Example: dog—hog.

pin	wig	pop	got	log
pig	win	hop	hot	dog

Exercise 8D

Here is a cockatoo. Draw his headdress on him on your paper.

Exercise 8E

Can you finish writing these?

Ant on an a __ __

Baby in a b __ __

Cat on a c __ __

Dog on d __ __

Eels on e __ __ __

Fly on a f __ __ __

Exercise 8F

Draw this girl on your paper. Write the words and put arrows to the correct parts of her body, like this:

shoulders	hips	knees	eyes	ears	nose	lips

WEEK 9

Exercise 9A

Draw the pictures on your paper. Say the word and listen for the beginning sound. Write the correct beginning letter next to each picture.

Exercise 9B

Fill in the missing letters. Write them in your exercise book.

Baby in a ___ed

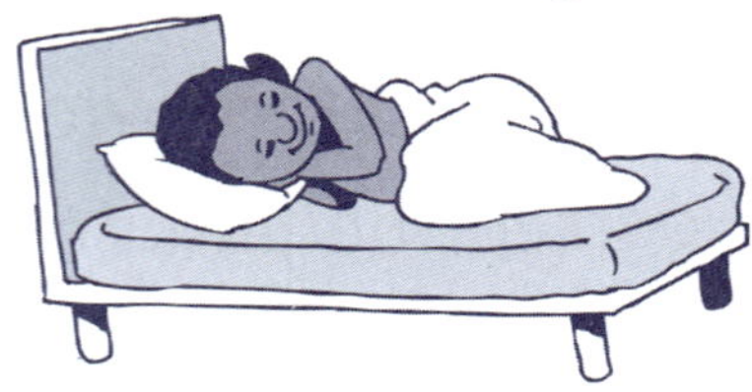

Dog on ___ad

Fly on a ___ish

Jellyfish in a ___ar

Rats on ___ocks

Whale on ___ater

Exercise 9C

What are the missing sounds? Write them in your exercise book.

h ___ t

v ___ n

d ___ g

n ___ t

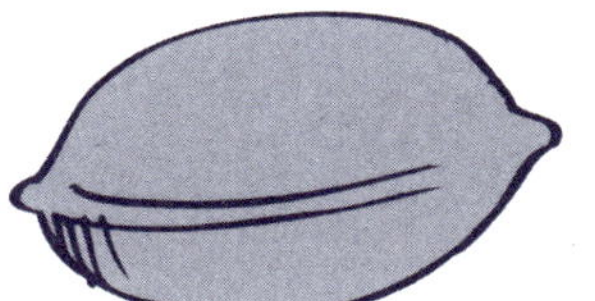

h ___ n

b ___ d

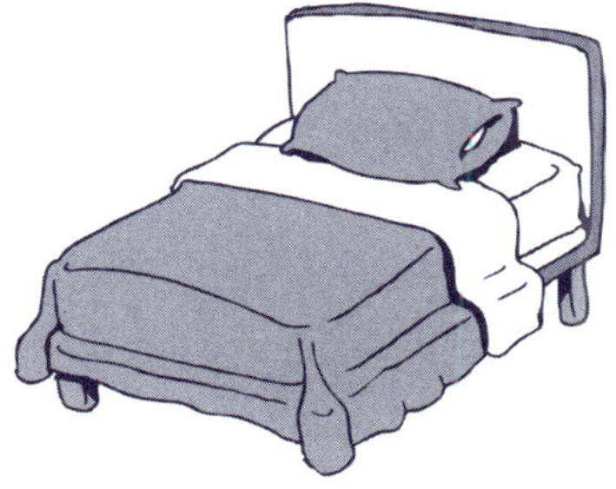

t ___ n

Exercise 9D

Read these sentences to a friend.

I went to the market.

I went to the hospital.

I went to the shops.

I went to the beach.

I went to the river.

I went to school.

I went to the village.

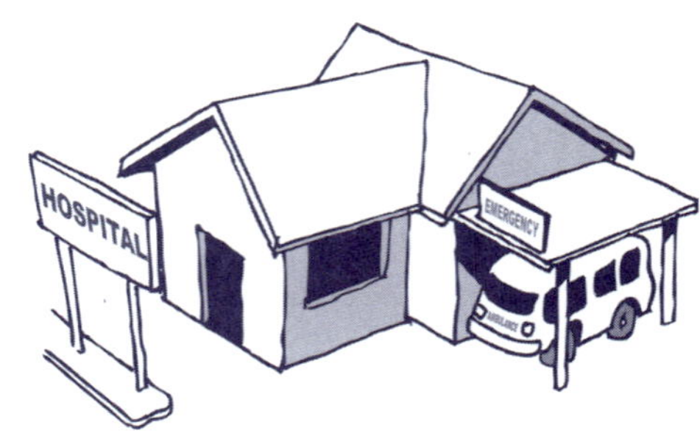

Exercise 9E

Draw these masks. Can you say their names?

pig

dog

lion

clown

mudman

King

Queen

monster

WEEK 10

Exercise 10A

Match these words with the pictures. Draw them on your paper.

yam	pen	net	bed	peg
pot	leg	log	gun	wig

Exercise 10B

Draw these pictures and write the correct sentence next to each one in your exercise book.

Ned's bed is red.

The pig is wearing a wig.

The man is in the van.

The cat is wearing a hat.

I can cut the nut.

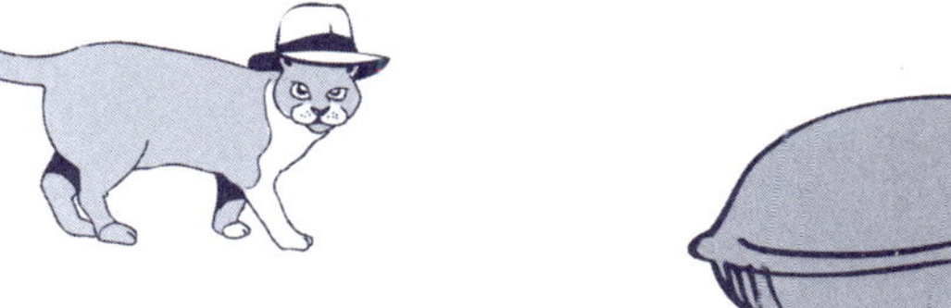

Exercise 10C

Draw the boxes in your exercise book. Find the words that start with these letters and write them in the boxes.

d	
p	

dig pip dot pin pot din dip pig

Exercise 10D

Read these sentences to a friend. Then draw the pictures.

Yesterday, we made Christmas stars.

Yesterday, we made Christmas cards.

Yesterday, we made Christmas trees.

Yesterday, we made paper chains.

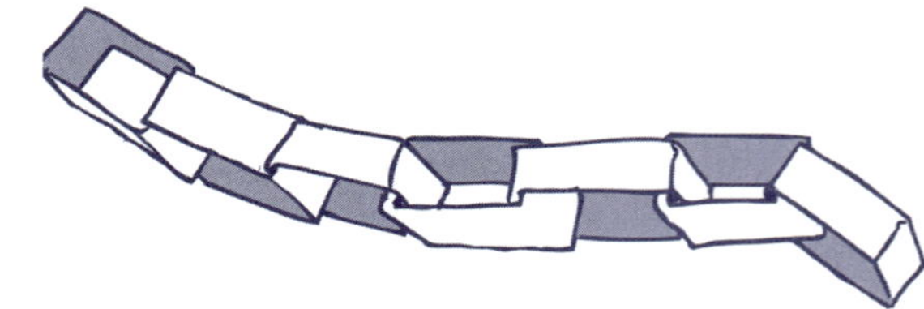

Exercise 10E

Can you draw this Christmas tree? Draw it on your paper with the decorations on it and the gifts under it.